EAST OF KATMANDU

BY THE SAME AUTHOR

Highland Days	Cassel	(1948)
The Ultimate Mountains	Cassel	(1953)
Camps and Climbs in Arctic Norway	Cassel	(1954)
East of Katmandu	Oliver & Boyd	(1955)
The Scottish Lochs Vol 1.	Constable	(1970)
The Scottish Lochs Vol 2.	Constable	(1972)
Western Highlands	Batsford	(1973)
Batsford Colour Book of the Highlands	Batsford	(1975)
The Scottish Islands	David & Charles	(1976)
The Scottish Lochs (Abridged into one volume)	Constable	(1980)
Tom Weir's Scotland	Gordon Wright Publishing	(1980)
Weir's Way	Gordon Wright Publishing	(1981)

PART AUTHORSHIP

Wild Life in Britain	Automobile Association	(1976)
Wildlife in Scotland	Macmillan	(1979)
In the Country	Macmillan	(1980)

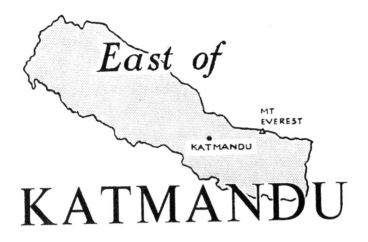

East of

KATMANDU

by

TOM WEIR

GORDON WRIGHT PUBLISHING
55 MARCHMONT ROAD, EDINBURGH, EH9 1HT
SCOTLAND

ISBN 903065 35 5

All photographs by Tom Weir

Printed and bound by
CLARK CONSTABLE LIMITED
EDINBURGH

Contents

Maps

In Memory of a Great Mountaineer

TOM MacKINNON

Died October 1981

INTRODUCTION

In 1965, exactly ten years after the first publication of this book I was writing at my desk when came a knock on the door of my Loch Lomondside house, and there before me when I opened it stood Sherpa Dawa Tenzing whom I had last seen in Katmandu as we said our farewells at the end of the expedition described within these covers.

Dressed in green tartan shirt, his jet-black pigtail wound about his head and secured with a neat pink ribbon, trousers tucked into his thick stockings, climbing boots on his feet, he was exactly the man I remembered, a bit more of a dandy perhaps. And as I moved forward to grasp his hands out from the wall stepped my fellow expeditioner Tom MacKinnon, who had driven him out from Glasgow. It was a jolly reunion.

Dawa was one of two Sherpas who had been brought to Britain on the invitation of Sir John Hunt and Sir Charles Evans for their outstanding services on the first ascents of Mount Everest and Kanchenjunga. Dawa, I should explain, was not the Tenzing chosen to make the summit climb with Hillary. He was one of the supporting four singled out by Hunt for extraordinary devotion to duty doing ". . . exceptional skilled and strenuous work with Lowe on the Lhotse". That quote comes from *The Ascent of Everest*.

Evans of course played a very big part in the Everest triumph, and when he was chosen to lead the attempt on Kanchenjunga, he appointed Dawa Sirdar of the Sherpas and Tom MacKinnon to be one of the climbing team, which brought a man from Glasgow and the forty-year-old Sherpa together again.

Dawa was to be our guest on Loch Lomondside for a few days and I found it strange indeed to be going around my home ground with a man of Tibetan origin, from a remote part of the world absolutely unknown to western people until 1950. Even in Nepal few within the boundaries of his country had heard of the Sherpa homeland of Sola Khumbu whose villages perch at 13,000ft, and whose people herded yaks, wrested a living from reluctant soil, crossed the highest passes in the world to trade with Tibet, and took themselves as far as Darjeeling to sell their labour to whoever would buy it.

It was a Scot, Dr A. M. Kellas, who was the first to discover that Sherpas were better porters than any other tribesmen when it came to Himalayan climbing. A pioneer explorer, Kellas was climbing higher and more often than any other mountaineer of that time and Kellas was the first man to die on a Mount Everest Expedition, of a heart attack at 17,200ft on the approach march in 1921.

In these early days Sherpas were porters, not companions. It took Eric Shipton in the mid-30's to discover this when he began a long association with the men of Sola Khumbu whose homeland still remained a mystery to him until 1951 when Nepal opened its door to the outside world and Shipton entered with the reconnaissance party which was to discover the route that took Sir John Hunt's party to the top.

The late Eric Shipton tells the story in his superb autobiography *That Untravelled World*. This is a fragment of it:

". . . . Waterfalls cascading down the huge precipices flanking the wide valleys of the Dudh Kosi, sparkled like threads of silver hanging from ice peaks 12,000ft above our heads.
We had reached Sola Khumbu, and our progress up the valley began to resemble a triumphal procession. I have never known such a welcome. At each village along the path all the Sherpa inhabitants, men, women and children, turned out to greet us, and we were invited, often dragged, into one of the houses for a session of *chang*-drinking. I met scores of friends from pre-war expeditions, and many others whom I did not recognise but claimed acquaintance. After a while I found it increasingly difficult to recognise anyone, and I marched along in a happy alcoholic haze."

Like Shipton, I was one of the very first Western travellers into a region close to the altitude limit at which man can live in precarious balance with his environment. Pressures were coming upon it from outside at the very time Dawa was visiting me, and they were causing him concern. Refugees from Tibet had crowded into the villages of Sola Khumbu. There was a military post in his village of Khumjung. The trade with Tibet in salt, wool and grain, vital to the Sherpa economy had been severed. Worst of all, a total ban had been placed on climbing expeditions in the interests of Nepalese security.

The Government was aware of the hardship caused by the banning of climbing expeditions, so they encouraged a new type of tourist who was unlikely to cause border incidents – mountain trekkers – eager to buy packaged deals advertising treks to the Everest Base Camp or around Annapurna. Flying into Katmandu the trekkers could be airlifted across the foothills into the grand scenery of the high country. The Government aim was to foster tourism and create employment for Sherpas. Brilliantly successful it was to have repercussions which my wise old friend Dawa was quick to see, because he was in the middle of the honey pot.

The old man had gone into retirement with the lamas of Thyangboche Monastery, whose marvellous position on the crest of a ridge looks on one of the finest mountain prospects on earth, not only on the near mass of Mount Everest a short marching distance away, but on a whole ring of ice spires. Just at the time of writing this sentence I had the good luck to read a modern mountaineer's impression in the Alpine Journal of 1981, by Simon Fraser. This is the extract:

". . . . the classic books on the subject do not really prepare one for the huge scale of the Everest massif, 'vast in unchallenged and isolated supremacy. . . .' Nor do they prepare one for the litter and environmental damage at Thyangboche, or for the sight of elderly Americans clad in down from head to foot, struggling with great fortitude to over 5000 metres while their leader 'Lord of all' like the mountains they have come to see, swaggers around the camp, NO PROBLEM inscribed in bold letters on his sweat shirt, giving orders to Sherpas and anyone else within earshot.''

No wonder Dawa wrinkles his nose in digust at the constant interruption of his prayers by tourists. Here are some words of his from Thyangboche in 1973. "Many people come; looking, looking, taking picture. Too many people. No good. Some people come, see GOOD!'' Dawa has observed that when tourists to Sola Khumbu can outnumber Sherpas two to one, and show an irreverent curiosity with bad effects on the local community, their presence is the opposite of good.

It was from a fine book by the Californian mountaineer Galen Rowell, published by Allen & Unwin Ltd. in 1980 that I got this quote. Rowell uses part of it for the title, *MANY PEOPLE COME, Looking, Looking.* His superb book is about high adventures in many parts of the Himalaya, but the two chapters which unravel the various threads which are causing disquiet to Himalayan mountaineers and the older generation of Sherpas are headed "The Coming of Age of Adventure Travel" and "Tourism and the Khumbu".

The problem is not only of numbers of tourists but of the disintegration of the community life of the Sherpas in an inflationary economy where it is every man for himself. You could say the natives are getting too like the tourists, even to the point of disregarding the conservation of the woodlands which is their only source of fuel for cooking and heat. Villages in the past rigidly controlled the gathering of firewood to ensure a continuing growth of timber. This seems to be no longer true.

Galen Rowell brings in Sir Edmund Hillary who has done so much to try and help the Sherpa economy by bridge building, constructing small airfields, piping water supplies and establishing schools and hospitals. Hillary confesses too his own careless plunder in the early days when fuel seemed limitless. He is quoted as saying. "You turned the corner at Pheriche and the whole place was a deep green, clothed in juniper right up the valley and beside the glacier everywhere. Well of course you have to look pretty hard even to see a single bush.''

He talks of the hundreds of porter loads carried up the Khumbu glacier by British and Swiss parties. Many more big expeditions have followed that trail since then. His end statement reads. "Now the juniper has been virtually wiped out. The whole area up there is just a desert now which is all eroding.'' Alas, that decimation spreading to the village areas means that local folk have to go further and further to get their fuel, including loads which they sell to the trekkers at an ever increasing price, even cutting it green which was previously forbidden.

The declaration of National Park status for Sola Khumbu in the mid-nineteen seventies has not cured this problem, which in fact has been aggravated by more developments to encourage trekkers, whose numbers are ever-rising thanks to over seventy firms in Katmandu who obtain their clients through over one thousand travel agents advertising adventure treks in the Himalaya all over the world. Perhaps with comfortable lodges all the way to the luxurious Everest View Hotel, only twelve miles from the summit of the highest mountain in the world as the raven flies or the aeroplane drones, it will eventually reach saturation point.

Yet this is not the whole picture. Trekkers and tourism cannot utterly deface one of the mightiest regions on earth, or touch the people of the remoter valleys. Yet I was amazed to hear that it is possible now to book a trek over the Tesi Lapcha described in this book. Even in 1976 trekkers were using it, as I know from an interesting letter from Mr Barry James of Ottawa, Ontario who had been attracted to the difficult pass by reading *East of Katmandu*. He wrote:

"At Beding (the very remote village in the Rowaling) we found a large party from a German mountaineering club had just passed through and were camped with their forty plus porters and guides, collapsible stools and tables, gourmet foods etc. We hired a young Sherpa porter, stocked up on corn tsampa and set off up the valley. The German party agreed to us accompanying them to the top of the Tesi Lapcha. We would leave them and go at our own pace from there."

He describes two camps on the way and climbing the icefall to meet a bitter wind on top and goes on:

"Some step-cutting and fixing ropes were necessary in the icefall, we camped about 500ft down the other side. It was a memorable night indeed, the Sherpas spending the night without tents, huddled around fires among the boulders at the base of bluffs."

He finished by telling me of other passes he and his wife crossed, travelling simply and carrying their own kit.

"In most instances it seemed that so very little had changed since the early fifties, but the new hotel above Namche Bazaar, the new airstrips, and many foreigners on the main paths around the standard trekking route to Everest Base Camp were an added feature to the world that you so vividly described. We thoroughly enjoyed your book and owe our trip over the Tesi Lapcha to your description."

And where had he got hold of the book? At Kalimpong in the dusty old library. They tried to get a copy of their own and failed, but got a read of it in the British Council Library in Katmandu. *East of Katmandu* has been reprinted because so many people want to have it. I have even heard it described as a classic, perhaps because it tells of a simpler world which will never be seen again.

Tom Weir

CHAPTER ONE

HORROR COMIC — THE BOMBAY CUSTOMS

SEPTEMBER; stifling heat and humid air; and we wilt in the Bombay Customs House, feeling that if hell has an earthly likeness it must be the interior of this dismal place of corridors, iron grilles, and inmates who sit at wooden tables trying to sort out a man-made inferno of regulations; papers that rustle in front of worried faces—Anglo-Indians mostly, who talk with Welsh-like accents, and who certainly do not intend to meet us half-way.

They want us to pay duty on 1200 pounds of food and equipment, and we have no intention of doing so. We are a Himalayan Expedition—or at least such is our grand title—and for the hundredth time, it seems, we give our reasons why we do not intend to part with the fabulous sum of rupees demanded. All they seem to understand at present is that we are Scots, and so they are determined to attempt the impossible by trying to take the breeks off a Highlandman.

For the umpteenth time we explain that we are the Scottish Nepal Expedition, that we are going to Katmandu to explore the region west of Everest, that our 1200 pounds of boxes contain merely tents, old climbing clothes, primus stoves and iron rations. Every item is listed, and since we have been granted 'duty-free' entry into India, and anyhow we are merely passing through India to get to Nepal, please can we get on, get out, and leave them to pester someone else?

There are four of us concerned. George Roger, who has never been to the Himalaya before and who makes the mistake

1

of using tact and diplomacy, conceding his points, hoping to do by persuasion what he cannot do by thrusting his case down Customs Office throats. George is a gentlemanly type from Gourock on the Clyde, and we watch with interest to see how long his reserves of good nature and politeness will take to break down under the strain of Indian inefficiency and unwillingness to make a positive decision on anything.

Douglas Scott and Tom MacKinnon are old companions of the 1950 Scottish Himalayan Expedition, men of patience and determination, who know when to stop smiling and get down to business; as for me, impetuous by nature and quick to anger, my impulse is to wrest our goods from the Indian Customs by any means in my power.

Our expedition is a democratic one, with no appointed leader. Jobs get done by someone undertaking them rather than by anyone formulating a plan or laying down an order. In fact there is something rather miraculous about being here at all. In June we had done nothing except mark time on getting a political pass into Nepal to explore—applying not very hopefully when Nepal first threw open her door on 500 miles of unexplored mountains hitherto closed to all generations of mountaineers.

Our luck was that W. H. Murray, who had been with us in Garhwal in 1950, had been chosen to reconnoitre the south face of Mount Everest with Eric Shipton, and thus was one of the first mountaineers to see a terrain shrouded in mystery until his visit. The party came home with a tale of a fantastic land; of spectacular gorges in whose depths travel was even more difficult than over the snowy passes to Tibet; of Sherpa villages perched in incredible places below the highest peaks in the world; of a mountain with the name of Amadablam supported on razor-sharp ridges and easily the most formidable peak ever photographed.

Their fascinating job had been to puzzle out the topography of the Everest massif, and find a route to the summit if possible. The splendid ultimate result of this reconnaissance is known to the world, but how many people remember the magnificent exploration achieved by this party which comprised Shipton, Ward, Murray, Bourdillon, Riddiford, and Hillary? Using glacier highways and crossing cols never before traversed by any human beings they explored east and west, seeing and naming great mountains, and finding footprints of the Abominable Snowman that excited the world.

What attracted us most was the description of a great gorge they had seen, a sheer-walled canyon called Rolwaling, into whose depths they had peered for 7000 feet, down an ice crest above a basin not unlike the Nanda Devi Basin, in the centre of which was a peak of pale granite and ice which they named the 'Menlungtse Peak.' The gorge at their feet was called 'Rolwaling' after the furrow made by the plough, and it was on the glaciers of this region that they found the prints of the Snowman.

That was in 1951. The plans we made in 1952 were to explore this gorge, and try to climb some of the magnificent peaks that Shipton and Murray had described so well.

In the Himalaya, of course, everything hinges on getting a political permit, a more difficult thing to achieve than the summit of many an ice peak, as we knew from our previous experience when in 1950 we had to set sail without it, and miraculously tracked it to earth once we were in India.

Waiting for the Nepal pass was interesting for me, because I had three strings to my bow. First was the Himalaya, but if no permit came through by June I had the option of a place on a sledging expedition to Spitsbergen. Then in May, while still waiting for the permit, I was invited to go on the British North Greenland Expedition to Queen Louise Land. Ad-

3

vanced stages of dithering were suddenly ended by the arrival of the permit. We were on—to Nepal—and there was not a moment to lose, because our application to explore was granted with effect from August to January, which left us only two months to prepare.

Hectic months—getting tents—buying food—arranging import and export licences—pulling strings to get boat berths to Bombay—working out a plan of campaign—then on the day of sailing for India to be told that there was political upheaval in the country and that all travel to Nepal was temporarily restricted. Can you imagine us returning home? Certainly not.

We sailed, and put all unpleasant thoughts out of our heads for the duration of that delightful voyage over 5000 miles of tranquil ocean.

Now in the Bombay Customs house it seems we are hammering our heads, not against a brick wall, but against something more rubbery, composed of ignorance and stupidity against which one only rebounds, and not even the United Kingdom Commissioner can batter through. But he brings us good news. We are being allowed to proceed to Katmandu; and to speed us on our way H.M. Government are prepared to act as guarantors that duty will be paid on our food and equipment if this is found to be necessary.

This should be sufficient for any Customs House. But instead of accepting it they now lay down a contrary policy, involving the relisting of all our stores under two headings, consumable and non-consumable, so at the end of another day we are no further forward, despite the fact that they know and we know that New Delhi has granted us duty-free entry of all our goods.

We have nearly reached the fighting stage by now, and violence is almost done when next day they demand yet another set of lists, with prices of every item this time. Even the

4

peaceful George recognises the last straw when he sees it, and when we go in a body to see the chief of the Customs House he wilts visibly at the sight of our outraged faces.

He listens respectfully, and we expostulate with as much arm-waving as hillmen deprived of backsheesh, and to our astonishment he does not even put up a defence. 'Enough,' he says. 'Tomorrow you can go.' And we do, pausing only a moment as we board the Frontier Mail—not to offer up a prayer for our deliverance but to wish the Bombay Customs House a soldier's farewell—and settle down for a tranquil night, or as tranquil as one can reasonably expect on a hot and heaving Indian train.

CHAPTER TWO

DELIVERANCE—KATMANDU

WE awoke on the plains, in the gold of a September dawn, and from the railway carriage window looked on swirling rivers in brown monsoon flood, gay with lines of snow-white egrets. India is in fact a land of birds, so numerous that they are a physical part of the landscape, in their grace, flashing colour and infinite variety, from grass-green bee-eaters and slim wren warblers to long-winged marsh harriers and hovering vultures.

The pleasure of being an ornithologist is that no country is ever empty for you, and to Douglas Scott and myself it was like coming among old friends to see little cormorants sunning themselves on high banks, wings outstretched like their larger brethren of the Clyde. Near and far we could see patient paddy birds, sombre-coloured like stones until they suddenly opened white wings and became graceful birds like miniature herons. In the air were glossy king crows and ragged kites flying high above the bustle of busy minahs, the latter like so many gay starlings. Kingfishers, pied or vividly blue and orange, dashed on whirring wings over the water. Blue jays, shrikes and bee-eaters occupied the telegraph lines for mile after mile.

The vastness of India! So much of it flat, green, empty of human life. Monotonous mile after mile until suddenly a weird rock escarpment breaks the unending landscape. Now and then there are lonely figures of herdsmen with cattle or goats or water buffaloes, or ploughmen plodding behind their labouring oxen on the sun-scorched plain. Humid air and wilting heat—hothouse greenness, so different from the dry dusty desert of May in the pre-monsoon period of our first Himalayan expedition, when the land was on fire and crying for water and we sat round a block of ice with the screens of the carriage drawn, as we do round our own firesides on a winter evening at home. How in such a climate can people live in shanty-town villages of tin huts like air-raid shelters, devoid of protection from the ferocious Indian sun? Living in these huts must be very much like being baked in an oven.

It is always a surprise to run into a railway station in this sort of country. Here, in contrast to the sleeping country, is hell let loose in babbling humanity—the cries of vendors, the whines of beggars, the slamming of carriage doors and the shouts of coolies competing for trade. When we reached Lucknow on the following day there were even acrobats and performing monkeys to divert the traveller and part him from his rupees.

We were on the last lap now to the Nepal border, speeding through an absorbing country of river, lake and flood water—a region where every tree had its growth of weaver birds' nests, and tall stalks of sugar cane grew thickly—rice and banana country, with fields of tall Indian corn so good to eat when roasted.

The long independence of Nepal was favoured by the notoriously unhealthy country that stretches north of the Indian railhead at Raxaul. What we saw when we got there was a dismal place of flooded rice fields and palms, dotted with sugar factory chimneys, occupying a plain only 350 feet above sea level, and with dismay we learned that we would have to spend the night in this hot and smelly place. There was no train to the Nepalese town of Amlekganj until the following morning.

The only highlight of Raxaul was a cold bath that washed away the sweat of two and a half days in the train. But we shall not readily forget the one night we spent in the Nepalese Rest

House adjacent to the station. Poor George Roger was not only bitten, it seemed to him by every known variety of insect, but when we went for a walk down the village street he was attacked by a monstrosity of a duck-goose that hissed at him, snapping with outstretched neck at his khaki-clad legs. And if George didn't turn a hair he was at least on the defensive with his umbrella.

He had further grounds for invective when we went for a meal to the station restaurant, which was dark except for an oil lamp on our table that attracted winged shapes from all points of the compass. George was tackling a curry of unappetising appearance, and as he lifted a portion of meat on his fork a large armour-plated insect like a buzz bomb exploded on his plate, wings flailing and drumming. Startled, he leapt back, then fell to the attack with his knife and fork, muttering savagely. Douglas's statement that it was 'only a dung beetle,' was scarcely mollifying, and George was in the act of saying so when a long green animal like a flying banana ricochetted off the table lamp to cannon from his neck on to the plate. And for the first time in our lives we saw him really ruffled as he sprang to his feet and grabbed his hat.

Outside we were confronted by an amazing sight. On the velvet blackness of the night darting lines of red were criss-crossing like some incredible firework display, or an infantry attack with tracer bullets. Not for a few moments did we realise that we were looking at fireflies tracing their movements within a few feet of our faces. We thought we were accustomed to the insect noises of the Indian night, but the chorus of cicadas and bullfrogs at Raxaul was the loudest and most ceaseless vibration of clamouring sound we had ever heard—an evil sound in the hot sticky air of that place. Above it we could hear the sound of a drum beating, and faintly in our ears—almost in echo of the whining of a mosquito—was the shrill voice of a woman singing

8

a wavering song charged with emotion and sex. There was no doubt that we were in the East. We retired to bed, but not to sleep, for the mosquitoes droned in our ears in weird harmony with that shrill song, and we had no nets to ward them off. We simply had to lie and be bitten.

That night an incident occurred that may have been real or imagined, for I had been reading a story by Jim Corbett about cobras and what I thought was real may have been the result of a dream. But I awoke in panic in pitch darkness with something slippery slapping my face, something that felt reptilian. My hand went to my face and at the same moment there flashed through my brain the thought 'a hooded cobra!' I tried to keep still to let it slide away, then gave the alarm.

Everyone was awake instantly. A light was flashed and I told my tale, but there was nothing to be seen.

'That is all I needed,' said Tom MacKinnon. 'I've had enough of this. I'm going to sit outside on a chair rather than lie and be bitten in this hell-hole.'

Tom and George got up and sat outside on the veranda. Douglas and I stayed on—and slept.

Next day we moved into Nepal, climbing gradually through rice fields into the Terai on a narrow-gauge railway. Times have changed since this was all unhealthy swamp and jungle. Reclamation has turned much of it into prosperous farm land and it is now renowned as the granary of Nepal. The rice harvesters were busy on their flooded fields, and on the pasture were herds of goats, pigs and water buffaloes. Houses of red clay with thatched roofs made neat little settlements.

Soon we were enclosed by jungle—the sal jungle which is said to be the haunt of elephants, tigers, panthers, leopards, black bears, wolves, jackals, wild buffalo, hog deer and four-horned antelope. The Indian rhino is supposed to exist here too, and it would be a bold man who would contradict the statement in

9

this kind of jungle; and it is to be hoped it is true, for with the passing of the Rana regime it seems unlikely that this teeming region will ever be hunted again on elephant back as of old, with hundreds of these beasts closing into a ring to trap everything contained in it. For six months of the year this is the most unhealthy jungle in India or Nepal, and the Tharus tribes which live within the forest would be extinct were it not that they are partially immune to a deadly brand of malaria known as ' awal.'

Quite suddenly we were finished with railways. We were at Amlekganj, and the train literally exploded people, all hell-bent on getting on to three ancient buses standing outside the platform. It was a battle of umbrellas, for the rain was teeming down, and the unfortunate ticket collector stood more than a little chance of having his eye poked out.

We chartered our own bus, a decrepit vehicle with tyres innocent of tread and windows patched with wood and paper. But though it rattled and vibrated alarmingly it went with a will into the lash of the rain and swirling clouds, climbing ever upwards, until suddenly we were in a ravine with chir pines askew on ragged crests above us—truly in the Himalaya at last. Grey langur monkeys with black faces crossed the road in front of us, absurdly friendly-looking to be considered Abominable Snowmen, as some people seem to think. Waterfalls poured from the hills and mud avalanches obliterated the road in places. Workmen were still busy clearing the latest of these where a vast slope of red clay sheered down to the river, and we had to wait while they cut an opening for our vehicle.

The roadway comes to an end at Bhimpedi, where a busy little town is compressed against the main wall of the Siwalik, the first of two mountain ridges barring access to the Vale of Nepal and the fabled city of Katmandu. The ridge rose above us as an uncompromising green slope cleft by gullies, up which we could

10

see a wavering path dotted with the bent backs of coolies. Theoretically we should have been able to get coolies from there to carry for us over to Katmandu, but not that night except at their price.

The old truth that every man is a capitalist was promptly demonstrated when the few nondescript characters available knew that we wanted to get moving immediately, and in ten minutes doubled their charges on their scarcity value. We were indignant and were telling them in no uncertain terms what we thought of them when we were rescued by a distinguished-looking native bearer in the employ of the British Embassy at Katmandu who urged us to leave the luggage to him. He would superintend its delivery to Katmandu.

How the Devil looks after his own! Such a piece of luck was not to be scorned, and though we were departing from the good rule in India of never separating yourself from your kit, we accepted his offer gratefully, relieved to be done with trains and buses and the gabble of wrangling tongues. To face a green slope and get some exercise, even if it was only putting one foot in front of the other, was the perfect antidote to the trial of patience which is the first test of the Himalayan traveller.

We were surprised to find ourselves climbing in the gathering darkness with speed and enjoyment, for first days in the mountains are usually a penance. In a steep village where drums were beating and men were singing we were directed to the Rest House, sited like a deserted mansion in splendid isolation. Someone from out of the dark took it upon himself to find the caretaker, and within half an hour we were inside, listening to the death cackle of a fowl which appeared on our plates in a remarkably short time.

What a contrast to Raxaul! Life there had been a sweat bath. Here at over 600 feet we were pleasantly cool—so cool that in lieu of bedding, which had not yet caught up with us, we had to don socks and pullovers to get warmth enough to sleep, and we did not need any lulling, for it had been a tiring and anxious day.

The air felt fresh as spring in the morning. Birds were singing and slow-weaving coils of mist drifted over jungle walls patterned with incredible rice terraces, built like staircases into the mountains. Far beyond the valley up which we had zigzagged by bus lay the Indian Plains—a pale as lavender sea stretching away to infinity.

It was a strenuous Himalayan march that lay ahead, twelve miles of ups and downs on a path whose boulders were worn smooth by countless bare feet—an Asiatic highway packed with scuffling goats and slow-moving buffaloes, strings of coolies bent under heavy packs, parties of Gurkha soldiers going and coming on leave, wealthy people reclining on litters or sitting perched in the huge baskets which are the taxis of this part of the world, powered by hill men and women who certainly earn their living the hard way. We had stepped into the seventeenth century, but for the giant funicular of an electric ropeway which spans the valleys, shuttling from hill top to hill top swinging baskets bearing trade goods from India, and (we hoped) some of our luggage.

As in Garhwal there were cunningly sited tea houses on the top of the steeper rises, designed to tempt the traveller to stop and buy a brass tumblerful of hot sticky-sweet tea at city prices of two annas a cup, and we only wished we could talk a common language to the round smiling Nepali faces eager to be friendly.

It was a stiff pull up to the ragged edge of the final pass, and it was with excitement that we climbed to its jungly crest to look across the Vale of Katmandu to Tibet, not to mountains but to towering banks of cumulus, a tremendous cloudscape that even as we looked flamed with sunset, filling the sky with incredible pillars of fire. On the plain below, tiny, remote, in the vastness of encircling ridges, lay Katmandu.

12

We stood spellbound, looking down on the twinkling lights of this last great city of Asia, as the turmoil of clouds deepened the encroaching darkness, swallowing up one by one the mysterious waves of ridges and valleys.

Below our feet was Asoka's Staircase, spiralling down a fierce jungle wall loud with the dusk cries of Himalayan barbets. (Asoka was the Emperor who in 261 A.D. proclaimed Buddhism to be the state religion of India, and established monasteries and temples throughout the land, himself becoming a monk.) We plunged downward on this 2,500-foot staircase, pausing not a moment either for breath or to pick off the leeches that attached themselves wherever they could, for it was a race with darkness and we did not know where we would sleep that night.

But we reckoned without the kindness of the British Embassy. Colonel Proud, the Second Secretary, had been notified of our coming, and had his men out patrolling to waylay us and bring us to his house. At the point where we joined the main path we were seized, whisked into a motor car and, rather dazed by it all, found ourselves with drinks in our hands, a hot bath waiting for us, and the best dinner we had faced for years. We had indeed arrived in fairyland.

CHAPTER THREE

DIPLOMACY AND DEMOCRACY

WE could scarcely have arrived in Katmandu at a worst time for travelling. Not only was the weather bad, but it was the eve of the greatest of all Hindu festivals, the Dassera, which is equal to our own Christmas, except that this season of feasting, blood sacrifice, dancing and ritual lasts ten days. We would be lucky if we could persuade coolies to forego these delights for the back-breaking work of trudging over the Himalayan passes in monsoon rain.

Such a setback gave us no immediate cause for alarm. Murray had told us of the monsoon difficulties with swollen rivers, leeches, hornets, deserting coolies, slippery paths, etc., so we were well content to wait in comfort rather than face the rain. Anyhow the historic event of four Scotsmen in Nepal called for diplomacy before mountaineering. It would be tactful to make a series of official calls, to the King's palace to sign his Visitors' Book, to visit his counsellors who had given us permission to explore, and to present our compliments to the chiefs of the new Government, reformed since we left home.

But the only sign of 'seething unrest' that had restricted travel to Nepal and nearly cost us our pass was a storm in a teacup, a political demonstration of about fifty young men shouting their heads off in the rain, taking advantage of the fact that the country was now a democracy. Before 1950 it would probably have cost them their heads to raise their voices against the Rana regime, which ruled with absolute power until it was overthrown by a congress party organised by a few hundred Nepalese.

14

We did not see the King, who as the reincarnation of the god Vishnu is still the figurehead of government, and polygamous by tradition, but we met his adviser, a young Indian by the name of Govind who occupied an office outside the white-pillared palace. In the name of the King we were welcomed to Nepal and offered the hospitality of the new democracy. The King, it should be mentioned, has never had any real power in Nepal, the premiership of the country having been vested in a maharaja.

Democracy was the word on all official lips. Its official dress was a dingy grey, with white pyjama trousers and a pillbox hat, in contrast to the red and gold uniforms which made the rulers of the old Nepalese kingdom the most splendid in the world. A former palace was now the Secretariat, but apart from that the Foreign Secretary might have been sitting in a London office, complete with telephone and filing cabinets, instead of occupying the room of a deposed maharaja. Matters of state were pressing, and the Foreign Secretary did not have much to say, but he asked searching questions in excellent English—how we had found entry into Nepal, and if our passes had been checked. Then, after he had spoken a bit about the new democracy, I had the pleasure of telling him that our expedition too was a democratic one, in that we had no leader.

Kugdamansingh, one of the King's counsellors, was one of the most interesting men we met. In his dress of coarse white trousers with shirt of the same material and white forage cap, he looked rather like a convict. And that may have been his intention, for he had spent most of his life in the maharaja's jail, languishing there for twenty-two years after plotting to blow up the seat of government with its ruler on it. Now he had his own mansion, an army guard to protect his life, and a position as uncertain as that of all the other rulers of Nepal.

But for the primitive rule of the old maharajas, he told us,

15

Nepal would not be a backward country but another Kashmir, with good roads and people from many lands bringing a rich tourist traffic to the country. Instead of filling the maharaja's pockets and keeping the people in a state of ignorance and subjection, the new Government was going to develop the country.

We listened politely and said nothing. After all it was 'progress' that had given us our chance of getting into the country, and we could not afford to be cynical, remembering that slavery continued in Nepal until 1925, and that only a hundred years ago there was a savage legal code of torture; murder and intrigue prevailed amongst its rulers until the beginning of this century. But we could not forget all the smiling faces we had seen since entering Nepal or the easy ways of the Nepalese, their comparative freedom from taxation, and their ability to spend four or five hours of each day in prayer or meditation. The price of material progress is too often to replace a smile with a worried frown, the god being money instead of inner peace.

There are three main towns in the central valley of Nepal: Katmandu itself, Patan and Bhadgaon; each is a wonderland of pagodas and temples, domes and shrines, narrow streets, slender pillars of gods and kings, bronze and ornate gilt carvings with woodwork delicate as lace. In Katmandu these oriental treasures are in contrast to the more recently built Gurkha city, appropriately built in the east end, as a monument to the power and wealth of the Ranas who became the ruling class after their conquest of the country and seizure of power in 1768.

Walking around it we found Buddhist and Hindu shrines with images of ochre-splashed gods on every corner. There are 2,733 shrines in the central valley, many of them worshipped by Hindus and Buddhists alike, for although most of the people are nominally Hindus they have not given up their original Buddhism, with the result that there is an astonishing complexity of beliefs and public celebrations.

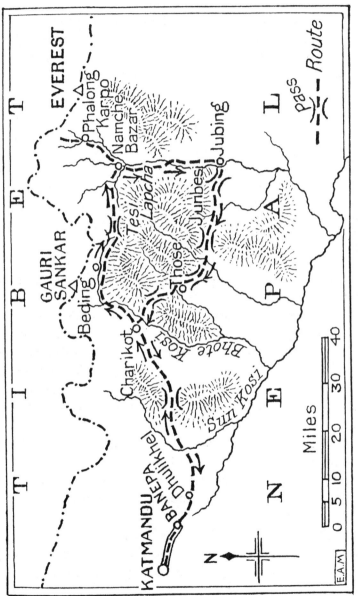

The route outward and inward.

At this time of festival the thriving activity in the peculiarly Chinese streets gave an air of vital life to the old Newar city of two-storied red brick buildings with carved lattice windows and wooden balconies. The little windowless shops and open bazaars seemed to be doing a roaring trade, and we saw nothing of the depressed look of long-suffering that is the common expression of the Indian masses. Men, women and children went about with smiles on their faces, delighting in the world about them. Gurkha soldiers saluted us, and some even gave us a 'present arms' of respect.

A vast trade was going on in animals for sacrifice, and round any corner we might meet with the severed head of an animal, for at the Dassera the thing from which a man gets his livelihood is worshipped in addition to his various gods. The soldier sets up his rifle and sacrifices a fowl or goat, splashing the blood on to the rifle. Even the lorry driver splashes blood on his radiator. After sacrifice the animals are eaten.

Motor cars are of course an anachronism in this atmosphere of the Middle Ages, especially as each one has been carried in bodily over the Chandrigiri Pass and set down in this flat land of the vale, but a jeep road from India to Katmandu has just been completed, and this will speed up the westernisation of this city, once so remote and now so closely linked by air with the outside world.

What did the Tibetans think of it, we wondered, as we watched a caravan drive their sheep into the Durbar square—men in pigtails, skin-clad, cloth-booted, sturdy, slant-eyed, broad-faced, in contrast to the smaller and more neatly dressed Nepalis who went about the city centre. For the Tibetans this would be journey's end—from the Tibetan plateau across a hundred miles of Himalayan mountains to this most fantastic corner of Katmandu, where on four sides there are the finest creations of a thousand years of oriental art, in pagodas, temples of richly carved wood, red-orange bricks, beaten brass roofs, slender pillars, steps bearing quaintly carved animals, a weird figure of the evil-looking god Kali. . . . What a contrast to the sprawling Gurkha city of hospitals, prisons, modern palaces, and crude statues designed in the nineteenth and twentieth centuries!

It was a very pleasing surprise to learn that our six Sherpas had arrived from Darjeeling—the first Sherpas we had ever seen. Not so small in stature as I had imagined, they advanced in a smiling body, and from their midst stepped Nyma, apparently the sirdar. His dress was European and his hair was cut in army style. He wore climbing breeches, top hose, climbing boots, and a gaberdine jacket over a smart pullover, and looked in general much smarter than most climbers of my acquaintance. His manner was cheerfully respectful. We did not know then that we were dealing with an unusually troublesome Sherpa.

Had we only known it, the real sirdar was Dawa Tenzing, Tibetan in appearance, with a long drooping moustache and shiny blue-black hair wound horizontally round his brow. Normally he wore it as a pigtail, and this horizontal winding was merely a concession to the sophistication of Katmandu. A red tartan shirt, R.A.F. blue trousers and smart brown shoes gave him a rakish appearance. Dawa, we were to discover, was the prince of our Sherpas, and was later to distinguish himself not only on the ascent of Everest, when he went to the south col, and later as sirdar to Hillary's 1954 expedition in the Makalu region, but also as headman to the successful Kanchenjunga team.

Mingma, Ela Tenzing, Ang Dawa and Kamin were the others. Ang Dawa was a good-looking youngster whom we at once nick-named 'the Boy Scout.' Although good at making omelettes he was to prove pretty useless in other respects. The truth was that he did not like carrying weights, nor was he fit for it. Ela and Mingma were first-class men, reliable types who

19

could climb and carry. Kamin was the youngest Sherpa, cheerful and good-looking, excellent around the camp but not an acquisition as a climber.

A pleasant piece of news was that they had brought four Sherpas from Sola Khombu who would act as porters for us. These were excellent young men, with one exception called Huma, a woman of uncertain age. How old she was we had no idea, but she was incredibly ugly and much attached to the tallest of the porters, whom I nicknamed 'Kharab Joe' because he wore a long-suffering, 'browned-off' look. Before the end of the expedition he was known to all Sherpas and sahibs alike as Joe, and a fine character he proved to be.

Coincident with the arrival of the Sherpas came news from the Embassy that the bearer entrusted with our precious baggage had seen it safely on its way, and that some of it should be at the terminus of the electric ropeway, while some of it was in his personal charge in Katmandu. This was great news, and with the Sherpas' help we rounded it up, doing some sleuth work among a mountain of gear at the foot of the Chandrigiri Pass. Only the kerosene had come to grief, though someone had ransacked a case and stolen Scott's best jacket.

Now we had something positive to do, sorting out loads and getting everything in order for the march, and after a good day we were invited to a cocktail party at the British Embassy at which the highest in the land were to be present, including B. P. Koirala, one of the two brothers who had led the revolution. Slim and distinguished-looking, young in appearance for his thirty years, he wore a khaki frock coat buttoned up to his neck and his legs were encased in tight pyjamas.

Most of the others wore finely woven jackets and waistcoats of semi-European cut over their fine silk shirts and pyjamas; pillbox hats were worn even inside the house. Most of the officials we had already met were present, but not the ex-convict.

Some seemed very nervous and neither ate nor drank; others talked incessantly in peculiar broken English and the word 'democracy' popped like a champagne cork out of every corner.

Even a beautiful little lady with pink roses in her jet black hair talked of it with flashing teeth. She might have been Japanese, except that her eyes were large and soft brown, glistening above high cheekbones. Her dress was like fine muslin with a pink sheen, only the tips of her white satin shoes showing.

A big surprise to us at a cocktail party was a lecture on 'Imagination in Literature,' given by a Dr Philips who had been flown specially to Katmandu. 'Kubla Khan' was the subject of his talk and he described how the poem came to be written under the influence of an opium dream. It was a good talk but it left us wondering how much of it got across to the Nepalese, for their command of English is not good.

Of outstanding interest to all our party was a meeting with Peter Aufschnaiter, the famous German climber who had been with Heinrich Harrer in Tibet after their epic escape from the internment camp at Dera Dun. They had been interned on their way back from a climbing expedition to Nanga Parbat, and about the middle of the war they escaped and made their way through Kumaon and Garhwal to Tibet, enduring incredible hardships and bluffing their way through the most difficult country in the world to Lhasa.[1]

As well as becoming civil engineer on water schemes and general improvement plans for Lhasa, Aufschnaiter was made official cartographer to the Tibetan Government and allowed to go into regions never before visited by a white man. He usually travelled alone, with yaks to carry his baggage. He told us that he felt completely happy in that country which he regards as the most fascinating in the world.

[1] The story is graphically told in Harrer's book, *Seven Years in Tibet.*

21

His eyes lit up and his rather solemn face became animated when he spoke of views he had seen over hundreds of miles of shining ice mountains, mostly unknown and unexplored. He had no wish to go back to Europe. His yearning was for Tibet, and he would never have left it if the encroaching Chinese had not forced him to cross the Himalaya into Nepal to seek sanctuary. His wish now was to find himself a job and be allowed to stay in Katmandu. He is now employed, I am glad to say, in the Vale of Katmandu by the World Health Organisation, and it is to be hoped that his plans for further exploration of the remoter Himalaya come to fruition. Already he was looking forward to winter and the arrival of trade caravans from Tibet, amongst which he would find many of his old friends.

So the first days of the festival passed in talking, being entertained, and parleying with the Sherpas, but no coolies were forthcoming. The men who might have been carrying for us were enjoying themselves, strutting about in the rain behind bands of drummers and musicians, and every night was a feast.

We had become quite resigned to awaiting the end of the festivities, since we could get no change out of any of the coolie contractors, when one of those unexpected things typical of the East happened, and we suddenly found ourselves with a crowd of ragged Tamil coolies to choose from, a small host having invaded our lawn. Yes, they were prepared to start right away, provided our loads met with their approval, so we let them loose among our gear, and after a deal of wrangling each man chose his load. We had the riff-raff of the bazaar without a doubt, but we were in no position to pick and choose, and our departure was timed for the morning. So we settled down cheerfully to our last night with Colonel Proud and the kindly staff of the British Embassy, who had done so much to smooth our path through Katmandu.

22

CHAPTER FOUR

ACROSS THE FOOTHILLS

THERE was a holiday feeling abroad and much singing and laughing as Sherpas and coolies packed aboard two ramshackle vehicles hired to take us far as the muddy road would allow. A grinding of gears and we were off. And how the Embassy staff envied us, for their duties are such that although they live in Katmandu within sight of one of the mightiest panoramas in the world, they can seldom get time off to go farther than the central valley.

We were heading north-east, to a destination which would be decided by the consistency of the mud on the road. Slithering and jolting, charging uphill, trundling through treacly mud, or winding between tall houses, we were doing well until the bus broke down. Undeterred we crammed everything and everybody on to the lorry which was our second string; there were thirty-six of us perched on top of the luggage, our position being precariously maintained as we catapulted along, ducking to avoid overhanging branches and climbing down to handhaul the vehicle from its frequent difficulties.

Our passage through the crowded street of Bhadgaon sent the people into shrieks of laughter as they scuttled for their lives out of our way. We literally scraped the walls of houses, swaying our way through the most famous city in Nepal for Newar art. We passed the most perfectly proportioned building in the East— the Temple of the Five Stages, its slender pagodas mounting slim pinnacle on slim pinnacle to a gilt top framed by a staircase of weird sculptured animals and orange-splashed gods.

Women in bright clothes washed beside a little lake, their reflections shimmering with those of the rich carvings of temples, while scattered beside them were bamboo mats of red capsicum-pods and yellow grain drying in the sun. The furious ride through this wonderful city, one new and striking scene succeed-ing another, was like the sequences of a technicolour film—we were spectators, not yet participants, though a loosened foot-hold or handhold would have pitched us very much into the scene.

Then the going got sticky and we had to get down and push— hard work which was made easier by help from passers-by— but it was amusing at each start to find we had gained some new passengers. Heaven alone knows how they managed to lodge themselves. One enthusiast for motor travel even rebuked us loudly because we would not stop and pick him up. At length we stuck beyond redemption, on the mud of a steep hill, and it was a relief to get out and walk.

It was raining now and streams poured from the low terraced hills on each side of us—streams black with earth washed from the upper slopes. Soil erosion is a continual process in Nepal, because no attempt has been made to conserve the natural timber of the upper slopes, with the result that soil is being con-stantly washed away. Many areas were as bald of soil as shale bings, the result of over-intensive cultivation and lack of timber conservation. We were to see this all over the lower foothills of Nepal.

A mile or two on our way there was a camp site on rain-saturated turf near a temple, and we put our first camp on it, in the midst of a gathering horde of spectators. Sherpas and Tamils vanished almost at once, and we did not see them again until morning. Evidently our coolies did not want to miss the festivities of the nearby town.

Heat and mosquitoes made sleep impossible that night, yet this was an advantage, for we were able to witness a unique spectacle—the Festival of the Lights. Through the darkness of the night there came the sound of drums and weird chanting. We were high above the valley looking downwards out of the tent when we saw snaking towards us a wriggling line of moving lanterns a mile long. The whole population of the town was marching to the temple to make offerings to the gods. All night long the people came in endless procession, accompanied apparently by all the howling dogs in Nepal. We were offered holy rice, flowers, and red kum-kum powder to dab on our brows.

The festival celebrations appeared to have been too much for our coolies. In the foothills it is particularly important to start early on the march, to make the most of the cool of the morning, which lasts until about nine o'clock. We were up before six, but at eight there was still no sign of our men, either Sherpas or Tamils. The fact was that they were naturally bad starters, as we were to discover during the next six days. Getting them going on the march was a daily trial of patience, for Nyma was quite useless at either taking orders or giving them. We would have given a great deal to have our old friend Kuar Singh of the Garhwal expedition to whip them to action and instil some discipline into the rabble.

However, we were lucky to be on the move, and luckier still in the weather, for the rain which we expected to make a penance of this approach to the Himalaya stopped after the first day, and for the next six days we had the pleasure of seeing an absorbing country instead of weaving a way through banks of dank monsoon cloud. In that time we dipped into steamy valleys, climbed over jungly ridges and contoured ravine after ravine in wilting heat.

What astonished us was the intense cultivation of these Nepal hillsides. Whole ranges of foothills had been scalped of every vestige of vegetation and terraced from top to bottom with green

25

rice and golden buckwheat, and everywhere on these monotonous staircases were the grim signs of soil erosion in avalanched
terraces and huge gullies riven out of wasted hillsides. Houses
were dotted everywhere and the paths were literally crawling with
people. The foothills of Nepal are not the place for an isola-
tionist.

It was nearing the end of September now, and it was interesting
to find that the distribution of birds was pretty much the same as
in summer, hoopoes and scarlet minivets being the finest birds
of the ridges to 7,000 feet, and by the streams at lower heights
were plumbeous redstarts, whistling thrushes and brown dippers.
Three black-necked storks among the banana palms of a valley
were a surprise though, as was a giant cactus in magnificent
white flower. Daily, above the ravines we were crossing, we
saw Himalayan black eagles, soaring birds easily identified by
their flight, dark colour and white patch on the rump.

We felt the sticky heat of these early days, and Tom had a mild
stroke of exhaustion which upset him for a day. A bathe in the
grey torrent of the Chak Khola was a life-saver for us all, in
water that was really cold, in a pool where we could lie with our
feet against a huge rock and let the fast-flowing current float us
back and forth while we languidly held up our umbrellas to
keep off the sun. A first bathe like this is a Himalayan memory
to treasure.

Each day the country grew wilder and our camp spots more
beautiful. The first sight of the snows was unforgettable. We
were camped on a green alp overlooking the deep trench of the
Sun Kosi and the Indrawati Rivers. Jungle ridge after jungle
ridge was softly outlined with gold under towering banks of
rose-coloured cumulus. The glistening wedge of a snow peak
projected above the clouds like a tent. No peak could be as
high as that! As we watched, spellbound, the clouds broke,
opening on a range of fantastic mountains stretching north and

cast to Tibet. That vision alone was worth a journey to the Himalaya.

A curious experience followed. We decided to sleep out and enjoy the bright light of the half moon in this magic situation. We spread our sleeping bags and lay down—but not for long! Ammunition was being spattered at us in the form of large blobs of stuff like tomato sauce. We heard thin squeaking sounds and saw the dim fluttering shapes of bats, criss-crossing in hordes overhead. One scored a direct hit on Roger's eye. They were fruit bats and we were getting their juice second-hand. Despite the bats and a broken night's sleep I thoroughly enjoyed the night outside, watching the clouds fill the valleys and lie in wavy billows on the dark hill ridges.

On another night we had an attack of a different kind when white ants got to work on Tom's waterproof and perforated it in the space of a few hours.

Blood-sucking leeches which we expected to be a pest were not too bad. These loathsome creatures are blind and like thin worms. Poised on a leaf or blade of grass they await their victims, attaching themselves to boots or clothes until they can wriggle through to flesh. They can thread themselves through the eye-hole of a boot and suck their fill of blood unnoticed. All of us suffered their attentions on arms, legs and feet, but the sores quickly healed despite our rough treatment of pulling the creatures off. The refined method of detaching a leech is to touch it with salt or a burning cigarette.

Despite the monsoon rain there had been only one difficult river to cross, and we considered ourselves lucky, knowing the difficulty that Shipton's party had experienced on their outward march from Dhankuta at approximately this time the previous season. I thought I was in luck this crossing, as I was lifted pick-a-back on a Sherpa, but he was an uneasy swaying mount, and we both nearly landed in the swirling river, so I took care to

27

cross every other stream under my own power. Himalayan streams flow with astonishing speed, and we had to make a coolie chain before we got the whole complement through its thigh-deep difficulties.

In Dr Longstaff's great book *This my Voyage* he answers the question, 'What must I do to become an explorer?' by saying, 'Qualify yourself. What a traveller gets out of any journey depends on what he brings to it when he starts.'

How little we brought to this particular journey we felt all too keenly. It was our privilege to be walking through a country which Longstaff would have given his right arm to explore. Everything we were seeing was new and vital, was fresh information to the world. Yet by not knowing a scrap of the language or customs of the people we were unable to interpret it. We were on the hill-top fringe now, where Buddhism and Hinduism overlap to such an extent that we could not tell whether the people had been Hindus first and Buddhists later, or the other way round.

What we did know was that the higher we climbed the less evidence there was of Hinduism. We had left the uniform region of terraced hillsides three days out from Katmandu, and now we were in a more mixed terrain where the houses were neater and cleaner, in pink and white wash, with thatched or wood roofs. Often there were neatly tended gardens growing in front of the houses, and the stackyards of Indian corn were neatly built and ornamented as in some farmyards at home. Usually the eaves of the houses were hung with corn cobs, and on high shelves round the walls were yellow pumpkins or green cucumbers, trays of red capsicum, or ripe grain drying in the sun. The people invariably gave us cheery smiles and invited us to sit down and pass the time of day with them. They were not Sherpas, nor valley-dwelling Nepalis, but hill people somewhere between the two in appearance and customs.

Mani walls[1] with sacred lotus flower carvings and groups of little pointed chortens[2] with Tibetan inscriptions were ever-increasing signs that we were coming into the land of Buddhism. Now, even although the hill tops were only 8,000 feet, we were among fluttering prayer flags nailed to staffs tall as telegraph poles and covered from top to bottom with the Buddhism prayer 'om mani padme hum.' The people of these hill tops regarded themselves as a cut above the people of the valleys and spoke of Nepal (only four marches away) as if it had been another land, for, strange as it may seem, the word Nepal, though it appears on maps of the world as pertaining to the whole country, means only the central valley containing Katmandu, so far as the natives of the land are concerned. A Sherpa from Namche Bazar thinks himself no more a citizen of Nepal than an Irishman of Eire thinks himself an Englishman.

Despite such a poor and straggling collection of coolies our march organisation was getting smoother and each camp spot was a delight. From the wood fires at night came the music of a shepherd's pipe, a contented melodious sound, simple yet with nostalgia in its trills and sustained low notes. We were getting to know the men and could jolly them on. Each day about mid-morning we stopped for tea, brewing up by some mountain stream, or taking advantage of a convenient hut to shelter from the sun, then sauntering on.

Huma, our only woman porter, amazed us with her energy. The men wore very little clothing but she was enveloped in her native homespuns of cloth a quarter of an inch thick. Bathed in sweat she would grin broadly if she passed us. She always carried an ice axe—whether as a walking stick or for self-protection we were not sure—and she was always humming a Tibetan song.

[1] Walls composed of carved stones bearing Tibetan prayers.
[2] Symbolic monuments representing lamist cosmology.

29

Somewhere, usually in the rear, limping and obviously not enjoying himself, would come Kharab Joe. He had made my luggage his personal responsibility and invariably grimaced as he passed, pointing to his neck where the frame of my rucksack annoyed him. His 'spiv' cut jacket and sleek black hair gave him the look of a 'corner boy,' and at this time we thought him a pretty poor specimen. I was to discover that he had a heart of gold, and was in fact one of the most delightful characters I have ever met.

There was a spring freshness in the mornings now. The sticky heat had gone and we were generally awakened by the whistling of jungle birds. By breakfast time, around seven o'clock, the low clouds would start to break up, and soon the sun would be glistening on every blade of grass of our ridge. Spectacular wads of cumulus usually stretched across the whole Tibetan sky, and if they broke formation we might see wonderful things.

Once from a ridge we saw the clouds split open and break into two wedges. Shooting up out of the clouds a great massif hung in the sky, ice arêtes and narrow corniced ridges glistening. During the nights we were bathed in moonlight, while the twinkling stars above us were answered by the flickering lights of fires on the vast hillsides where these hill folk lead their happy lives.

Tom MacKinnon was in his element now that we were really among the hills, and so was George Roger—the pair of them are life-long friends with mountains as their first love. Usually they were to be found together, striding well ahead of the caravan, botanising, conversing or photographing. Usually Douglas Scott and I travelled alone, birdwatching or selecting vantage points for pictures. But we always caught up with the others in time for morning tea. George would be lying contentedly enjoying the landscape while Tom, his umbrella tied to a stick to keep the sun off, would be scribbling furiously in his diary, for he liked to write his previous day's entry on the march and so have as much time to himself as possible in camp.

There would always be something to discuss: the ploughing and reclaiming of a hillside with oxen and matchets, or a strange black and white bird at a stream that turned out to be a little forktail, or maybe a falcon we had all noticed, gliding between rapid wing-beats, its ebony-banded tail transparent as an ivory fan. Tom might have gathered a posy of the attractive little flowers which grew on the paths to point out the various species to us.

On the eighth day out from Katmandu we reached the turning point of the expedition, at a meadow where the foothills stopped, and ahead of us rose the ravine of the Bhote Kosi mounting into the clouds of Tibet. For our Katmandu coolies it was their journey's end, but to our surprise they were now as keen to stay on with us as we were to get rid of them. The first thing to ensure before dismissing them was that we could in fact get other coolies at Charikot. This proved no difficulty at all, for as soon as we made our wants known a body of tough-looking Gurkhas with kukris in their belts was immediately forthcoming, ready to start off in the morning if we wanted them to.

Now we could relax and sit quiet, savouring the magnificence of this meadow perched so high above the Tibet River. How deceptive the country ahead appeared, smoothed into a misty blue in an over-simplification that denied the existence of the fierce tangle of ridges and gorges between us and the frontier ridge, which just showed as silvery spears pointing above the monsoon cloud filling the northern horizon.

The day after tomorrow we would begin the advance into this inner Himalaya, towards this territory some of which was blank on the map and inscribed with the single word 'unsurveyed.' The great thing was that all four of us were one hundred per cent. fit, a blessing in a country where it is all too easy to get pole-axed by dysentery or hill fevers. We were eating well and thoroughly enjoying life. The medicine chest had not even been opened, and that was sufficient testimony to our well-being.

CHAPTER FIVE

ROLWALING — INTO THE GORGE

THE twin points of Gauri Sankar stood clear of cloud over the Bhote Kosi when we looked out next morning. Distances had suddenly shrunk. The blue monsoon haze had vanished overnight and we could see the plastic gleam of ice on hanging glaciers and snow cornices curling on the tops of peaks that seemed incredibly near. It was truly the end of the monsoon, for the mountains of cumulus which had swirled round the peaks day after day had magically vanished. To the northeast we looked at peaks well inside Tibet, one of them being the massive square of Eric Shipton's Menlungtse peak.[1] To the right of it was a curtain of ice which we later named Rolwaling Wall, for we discovered that this impregnable wall was the frontier ridge of Tibet above the far end of the gorge some eight marches from where we stood. Under it we were to fix our first mountain camp.

Tom, George and Douglas went away climbing. I stayed in camp to write, to try and capture the many events of the past week. But there was not much peace. Charikot, being on a main route to Tibet, has a Nepalese Police Post whose function is to keep watch on all movements up and down the valley. The captain of the post wanted my credentials, and having examined them seemed unwilling to go. We understood each other in Hindustani and became firm friends. Half the population of Charikot village stood round gaping at these proceedings as he laboriously copied our names into his book.

[1] Named by the Everest reconnaissance expedition of 1951.

He also gave our coolies a pep talk, telling them that they would be answerable to him if we were not absolutely satisfied with them. We were paying them the same as our dismissed Katmandu men and he thought that we were much too generous. Actually they were well worth what we paid for them. So keen were they to start that many came that night and slept by our fire so that they would not be late in the morning. This was indeed a change. It revealed to us the true reason why we could never get a very early start.

That reason was the Sherpas, Nyma in particular. When our Charikot men were all packed up to go in the morning he was sitting sleepy-eyed over the fire with his companions, cooking breakfast. And what a breakfast—tea, rice, chapatties, tsampa, even potatoes. Not only were the Sherpas last up in the morning but their elaborate breakfast took four times as long to cook as anyone else's.

We left them at their breakfast and made off, hoping it shamed them. We dropped swiftly to the Bhote Kosi on a path steep as Ben Nevis for over 3,000 feet. The change in the country in the space of an hour or two was startling. Bluffs wooded with green chir pines became steep rock ribs dropping to the broad glacier river which curved below in a series of noble sweeps. White houses were perched in little corries above the gorge walls, and on every flat place by the river there were irrigation channels carrying water to flooded fields of tall brilliant green rice.

The valley of the Bhote Kosi was a feast of varied colour and alive with birds. The check that man imposes on bird life in the Himalaya by his over-intensive cultivation was evident. Here among so much natural jungle were chattering flocks of babblers, white-crested laughing thrushes with bibs to match their crests, fantail warblers, dainty little white-eyes (so named because of their conspicuous white eye-rings), yellow-cheeked,

34

red-headed and Simla black tits, blue rock thrushes, vivid
sunbirds of red, blue and yellow, curved-billed flowerpeckers,
fairy blue birds, nuthatches, woodpeckers, and a host of others.
This was the beginning of the real bird country. At every hour
of the day there was something to be seen, even families of red
and grey monkeys among the trees.

News travels fast in Nepal, and we had barely reached the
floor of the valley when we were intercepted and taken to a
house. Waiting for us here was a group clustered round an
important invalid who was their headman. MacKinnon, who is
a pharmacist in ordinary life and a very capable amateur doctor,
examined him. Apparently the man was on a starvation diet,
for diabetes was suspected. He complained of sore bones, a
sore head and constipation.

'The man is being starved,' said Tom. 'That is why his bowels
are not working, and he is tired because he is not eating. A
little meat, plenty of vegetables, milk, cheese, but no raw sugar,
are what he needs.' And so effective was his prescription that
when we passed this place a couple of months later the man was
fit and well. Tom hated the responsibility of making these
decisions in case the invalid should die of his treatment, but he
has never yet failed to cure. And he was to have an even more
spectacular success before the expedition was over.

We moved on in the heat of the day, and as we were now
down to only 3,000 feet above sea level it was hot, but to com-
pensate for the heat the river was at our side, and all we needed
to do when we felt like it was to plunge in and have a bathe.
But we preferred the side streams which were clearer and less
dangerous than the glacial rush of the Bhote Kosi. Our best
memory is of one ice-cold pool where the cataract swirled the
water in such a way that one got caught up in it, to be swept
in an arc to the far side of the pool, then borne swiftly back to
the starting point.

Soon we were clear of all signs of cultivation, on a path that contoured gently through the pines, reminding us of Garhwal, and the Girthi Gorges in particular, especially where the path had been washed away by a landslide, and we crept along on steeply inclined boulders and debris above the roaring river. Now and then we glimpsed the snows through an opening in the forest, or saw them standing high above wild rocky crests. The thin wild notes of the whistling thrush sounded above the torrent, sending our thoughts to the Rishi, for if the Rishi has a song it is the song of the whistling thrush. Bobbing on the stones was another familiar bird of the wild places, the white-capped redstart. How the sight and sound of these familiar birds so interwoven with pleasant memories added to the enjoyment of that day!

Below us everywhere we could see a selection of superb camping places, but we did not want to lose height and kept on, much to the disgust of the Sherpas, who believed that every working day should start at nine o'clock and finish at three, with enough time between to enjoy a drinking party at any convenient chang-house.[1] As it turned out, we found a magnificent place in the jungle where our new coolies instantly made themselves at home, fashioning a good shelter from trees hacked down with their kukri knives, and in no time at all they had fires going and their meal cooking.

Douglas was like a man intoxicated that day, he was enjoying it so much, and came in long after everyone else, almost inarticulate with the sheer scenic beauty of the place and the birds he had seen. Our camp fire was the last touch needed to complete the day for him, for above all things he loves a good-going blaze in the darkness of a forest. It reminded us of Dibrugheta, and the fire we had in that most delightful spot in the heart of the Rishi Gorge. Tonight, as in the Rishi Gorge,

[1] Chang is a rough kind of beer.

there was the same feeling of expectancy on the edge of the unknown.

The Charikot men were up and had eaten before our Sherpas would stir. It was annoying to have to begin such a perfect day with a row, and Nyma's excuse this morning was that Kamin was unwell. We were sorry for Kamin and arranged for his light load[1] to be carried by someone else, but we could not hold up our whole party on that account, so we left them sitting and hoped that the penalty of having to carry their own cooking gear would make them move more quickly next time.

They could catch us up or desert for all we cared, for the Himalayan mornings are the hours to treasure, when the air is crisp and cool and the birds are singing. This morning Gauri Sankar blocked the green defile of the glen, its lower rocks glowing warmly at the first touch of the sun and its snows glistening with a soft sheen.

The first problem on that spring-like morning was the Ghumbu Khola, which is a deep mountain stream so fast-flowing that no man can cross it unaided, though holding hands two men can race across its bouldery bed.

From here we took a path that was not the normal one—a narrow track over a rock bluff hung with waterfalls, one of which dropped 1,000 feet sheer in a ribbon of glistening foam. Sprays of orange flowers made a natural garden, the only snag being the brown threads of leeches waving like caterpillars on leaves and grass, waiting for a victim. The first indication that a leech has attached is a slight itchy feeling, but the warning comes too late, for by that time it has taken its fill of blood, and if it is trapped inside your stocking the thing you shake out is a blown-up body like a fat snail.

---

[1] The Sherpas refused to carry coolie loads except while actually mountaineering.

The charm of that jungly traverse made up for the attacks of fleas and ants and the bites of unknown crawly things which raised lumps on us. The end of the monsoon is a time of festival not only for the natives but also for the bugs; and fine as the ravine was, we were looking forward to getting on to the heights.

The placid George was on the warpath that night, and it was with surprise that we heard his voice raised in wrath. He spoke in English but his meaning was unmistakable, even to the Sherpas whom he was berating. His ice axe which had accompanied him on so many Alpine climbs had been nearly burned through on the shaft, and he had actually caught them using it for lifting pans from the flames of the fire. Now it was so seriously weakened that it would be no use for climbing.

'I call it a bad show, a damned bad show,' he was saying. 'It's not good enough, Nyma. If a Sherpa can't be trusted with an ice-axe he can't be trusted with anything.'

The axe was not the only thing damaged, for the Sherpas showed the same carelessness and lack of intelligence with the tents. We had been on the go now for nearly a fortnight, yet they either could not erect their tents or did not care how they erected them. One had a big rip in it caused by their not fitting the interior poles properly, and our own bungalow tent was ripped for the same reason. We could only conclude that the Swiss, who were then engaged on their second attempt on Everest, had the pick of the porters and we had the riff-raff.

How wrong we were we realised when we got rid of Nyma and appointed Dawa Tenzing headman. All they needed was a leader, capable of giving and taking orders. Nyma went against us at every turn, and our greatest mistake that trip was not sacking him there and then. We did not know it but there was a great enmity between Dawa Tenzing and Nyma. Dawa was biding his time, I suspect, and giving Nyma enough rope to hang himself.

38

Visitors arrived while we were looking at our bird books to check over the day's findings. It was dusk and the fires were blazing and crackling, and from nearby caves came the singing of our Charikot men. Quite suddenly the camp was invaded by a Bhotia caravan from Tibet—wild-looking men in rough home-spuns, with long pigtails and broad faces with high cheekbones. They crowded round our books and stared at the illustrations, making exclamations at species they recognised and pointing to the river if it was a river bird, or the trees if it was a forest bird, or the hills if it was a hill one. If the species was new to them they shook their heads. We were astonished at how many species they claimed to recognise.

Although we saw plenty of birds we saw little in the way of animals, though the high woods were supposed to be full of bears. We saw snakes, thin yellowish types that wriggled off the path at our approach, but we had no luck with tigers or leopards, wolves or deer, though we knew they must live in this wild region.

The importance of local knowledge Douglas and I realised one day when we came to a great boiler plate dropping sheer for hundreds of feet and curtained with a waterslide ending in a crystal pool—just the place for a bathe. We brushed our teeth, had a wash, then dived into this marvellous pool, looking up to a rainbow mist formed where the sun shimmered on the spray thrown out by the waterslide. We floated and kicked delightedly but were drawn back to earth by a man shouting anxiously to us.

Tactfully he withdrew until we had wrapped towels round ourselves, then he indicated that we should clear out quickly because stones were continually falling off the cliff above. If we had only looked carefully we should have seen the danger for ourselves, for the hillside was littered with stones, though most of them were thrown so far out on the hillside that we probably should not have been hit while we were in the pool. This friendly Sherpa was unusually solicitous for our welfare, and knowing that we were far behind the main column escorted us to a path junction in case we should lose ourselves on the rock slabs.

In four days of marching on narrow tracks—sometimes on mere ledges on the mountain face, sometimes high above the river, sometimes in jungle, sometimes on rock slabs, splashing through side streams, or gaining the opposite bank of the Kosi by swaying chain bridges slung high above the grey river—we advanced up a narrowing ravine to come face to face with Rolwaling. This was certainly a different proposition from anything we had seen so far. The scale was bigger, the edge of the gorge forming a huge bluff walled with plant-covered rock slabs which sprayed us with continuous rain as we approached under them. The route outflanked the ravine by climbing up 4,000 feet of this remarkable bluff, and already we could see the small dots of our coolies crawling on it.

There is a bridge across the Bhote Kosi at this point, rather a remarkable structure. A boulder the size of a house splits the torrent into two streams of boiling foam. From each high bank tree trunks have been thrown out to it and fitted with hand rails. They sway as you cross, and the few people we saw on the bridge prayed as they crossed, for the fate of anyone who took a high plunge off that bridge into the stormy waters below would be well and truly sealed.

We were surprised to find the wall above us spanned by a good path, climbing up a stony gully in the face at first, then winding up a ridge. Though there was no danger, the downward views were like those from a skyscraper—to the river like a silk thread twisting and twining ever upward to Tibet, towards Tingri where a rock peak stood on the frontier.

For 3,000 feet the slope was unrelenting, then we came to the terraced fields of a village situated in a fold between forest and crag, the village of Semgaon. At the first house Douglas and I were invited to enter, and a mat was spread ceremoniously for us to sit on. The man and woman were more akin to Nepalis than Bhotias in appearance, and they bustled about preparing bowls of sour milk and cream cheese for us.

This was the first time we had been in one of the native houses. There were two rooms, pink-washed on walls and floor. Bamboo mats laid with rice and wheat were spread to dry on the floors, and in the centre were the three stones which make a stand and fireplace for the curved brass pots and basins which are used everywhere in those parts. There was neither furniture nor carpets, though I suspect that these were kept upstairs with the wooden chests in which hill people store their treasures. The couple had five young children and were very proud of them. Without any self-consciousness the woman plucked up the youngest and gave it her breast while she smiled at us, in compensation for our not having a word of common language.

The Charikot men caught up with us here and indicated that this was not their sort of country. It was too wild and steep for carrying loads, they thought. The Sherpas thought it was time to camp but we did not. Our idea was to get the men up yet another thousand feet, away from the village and any thought of turning back.

It was the grand old man of our party, the oldest Charikot coolie, who got the whole band up a further thousand feet. We respected and liked this coolie, who must have been nearer sixty than fifty, and he knew it. He put our interests before his own at all times, and without complaint he shouldered his burden and started to climb with us. Rather astonishingly everyone followed. We had seen nothing of Tom and George all day and our suspicion was that they were already high above, in possession of a good camping site for us.

As it happened, they were high above us but not in possession of a camp site, for they had failed to find one. We were luckier, in that we found a little shelf in the jungle near a stream. Beside it was a little hut which the coolies piled into. Tom and George had contoured right over the bluff to look into the heart of Rolwaling, into a ravine even wilder than the Rishi, Tom said. Towering straight out of it was Gauri Sankar, so close that the vision had quite awed them, but not to the extent of stopping them from planning a likely route on it.

We judged our height that night to be about 10,000 feet, and for the first time forsook our light cotton bags for our eiderdown sleeping bags. As this was a ceremony which was not to be performed without ritual, we first examined our persons for fleas. Douglas got the best bag, with a louse, but we were content with lesser game. Determined to rid ourselves of these things we sprinkled ourselves and the bags with D.D.T., which proved effective, except against invading leeches.

The Sherpas were now having a private little festival of their own. In the village they had been on the chang, which was one of the reasons why they did not want to climb farther. They wanted to be on tap with it. Not to be outdone, they had carried a supply up with them, and were now at the giggling and singing stage. Tom liked this native beer, but the rest of the sahibs found it too thick and grainy to be pleasant. Its rather milky appearance rather than its taste put us off, but Tom has the faculty of being able to eat or drink any item of food peculiar to the country he happens to be in. The Sherpas on the strength of the local brew sang and danced, linking arms and stamping out their Namche Bazar rhythms to a late hour.

There was a request next morning that we get our gun out for the traverse of the thick forest clothing the face above us. 'Bahut balu,' said the men, meaning that there were many bears, so there was nothing for it but to get out the bits of our collapsible shot gun, a weapon so puerile and rusty that its only effect if fired at a bear would have been to blow some of its hair off and make it very angry indeed. Thus our fervent prayer as we marched ahead of the column was that we would not meet any, for the bang of our gun would spell disaster for the morale of the party if not death to some of its members.

Tom and George had prepared us for something spectacular in the first view of Rolwaling, but the thrill of stepping round a bluff and suddenly finding the gorge opening before us stopped us in our tracks. 14,000 feet above us—so close that we could see the texture of its hanging glaciers—was the wall of Gauri Sankar that had been our signpost for so long, a curtain of ice dropping to the wooded depths of a ravine filled with the golden light of morning; each tree gleamed softly on its sheer walls and waterfalls spouted in a sparkling spray.

The coolies prayed. Our own emotions were more complex, for the fluted snow cornices, jagged rock buttresses and incredible perpendicularity of this mountain were a kind of climber's nightmare. Nowhere else in the world perhaps do the horizontal and the vertical collide with such dramatic force in a plunge from the arctic to the tropical.

We had hoped we might find a route on this peak, and we were ideally placed for reconnaissance on this opposite side of the gorge, but we could see that the difficulties of getting on to its west ridge were far beyond the time at our disposal. It was a gorge problem as much as a mountaineering one, for the only ravine giving access to the west ridge was a formidable Rolwaling in itself—a tangle of trees, earthy cliffs, waterfalls and bare rock. But the ridge itself did not look impossible, though it looked long and steep and was protected by rock peaks which would have to be climbed if we were to reach it from the inner gorge.

Later on in the expedition we saw that a much better way to the summit would be up the north ridge which rises from the

Rongshar Chu in Tibet. This route is steep near the top but the angle is uniform and reasonable most of the way. With Tibet and the Rongshar Chu closed to Europeans there seems no alternative to the west ridge, and it would be a wonderful objective for a strong party, for there can be few finer mountains in the Himalaya than this isolated peak. (An attempt was made in 1954 by Raymond Lambert with a Swiss party, and the mountain was examined this year by a five-man expedition led by Alfred Gregory.)

We were in a region of blackened tree trunks between 150 and 200 feet high, gaunt skeletons of spruce or fir, burnt by some tremendous lightning storm perhaps but still standing. A secondary forest of young bamboo grew round them, sometimes sheered by landslides or intersected by dangerous rock slabs on which a narrow path led across notched tree trunks held to the mountain by wooden stanchions. This slender path was not always easy to find, and the coolies made a great noise to give warning to any bears that might be feeding nearby. Bears are not offensive as a rule but they attack without warning if taken by surprise. Our men were taking no chances.

In the jungle we met some Sherpas camped in a clearing with their yaks and wild sheep dogs. Salt from Tibet was out drying on mats in the sunshine, and we were invited to drink some yak milk simmering in a bowl in front of a fire. We would have been delighted to accept but for the stench of dung and the buzzing of hordes of blue flies that gave us no peace. This party of Sherpas had crossed a high snow pass from Tibet a few days previously and they were still suffering from the effects of glare and sun which had stripped the skin from the faces and lips of some of them. They shook their heads sadly at the memory of the unpleasant crossing.

It was necessary to be careful when descending some of the staircases built on the cliffs—one was made up of hundreds of solid trees rolled against each other, and they were slippery and damp. I slipped off one and fell about six feet. In another place I could have fallen a few hundred feet. I was more careful after that.

But there was only one really bad portion, where a landslide had swept away all vegetation and left a slippery wall of hardened earth. The Charikot men made light work of this dangerous and steep place but did not disguise the fact that they did not like these wild mountains. They looked at the ice walls above them with distaste, but there was no grumbling.

At two o'clock in the afternoon we were down in Rolwaling, on the floor of the gorge beside a deserted hut with plenty of firewood to hand, an ideal spot to camp, and we celebrated by having a dip in the ice-cold glacier torrent while tents went up and the coolies got snugly settled in the hut. The Charikot men did not waste their afternoon. Bamboo was all round for the gathering, and they lost no time in getting to work with their kukris, some gathering the bamboo, some splitting it up into long canes, and some making long baskets with the prepared strips. These large baskets are the rucksacks of the Himalaya and are used for transporting everything from human beings to loads of grain.

Rain fell heavily in the night and the snow line had crept down when we looked out in the morning to a wintry scene. At the head of the glen snow-plastered crags rose to cloudy gloom. Everyone was cold and lackadaisical. but the sun broke through with warmth and sparkle, sending spirits up again, and soon we were on the move with everyone laughing and singing.

We were agreed that the next few miles gave us the finest Himalayan march we had ever done. In the space of a few hours we moved from summer green through a feast of autumn colour into winter. The transformation was swift, as bleached skeletons replaced living green pines alive with birds. Threading a way under overhanging pinnacles, edging craggy corners, we followed the torrent into a wild version of a Highland glen. We literally stepped round a bend into autumn, into a paradise of red and yellow leaves where beards of grey moss trailed on the branches and Virginia creepers draped their flowers on the tree trunks. Glossy red berries hung everywhere and the coolies plied us with them, though some tasted like carbolic soap. Peeping out from the vivid vegetation underfoot were gentians, not dark blue but bright germander, matching the brilliant shade of the Tibetan sky, each with a little red iris in its open eye. They seemed to shine out of the ground and were wonderful heralds to announce that we were truly in the alpine zone.

On our left flank was a fretwork of rock pinnacles leaping up in mossy slabs to a comb of teeth. On the right the jungle thinned out in an upward sweep of 2,000 feet, the topmost layer crimson, each successive layer its own subtle variation of that colour. Swirling cloud, softening outlines and playing hide and seek with the sun, increased the impression of a Highland glen.

Then suddenly in the heart of this wild place we came to terraced fields, so small that you could hardly have pitched a tent on them. Beyond them the gorge opened like a door on to a flat meadow with a tall Buddhist chorten standing at its entrance. We were at our destination. Perched under the cliffs of Gauri Sankar was a huddle of houses, the Rolwaling village of Beding, the last human settlement this side of Tibet. It was the setting of a Shangri La, complete with lamas, for these religious men are the main occupants of the village.

They lost no time in getting acquainted, smiling all over their broad faces as they came down from their boulder-like houses to greet us. They were all dressed in the red homespun robes of their priesthood. Children with bright rosy cheeks flocked round us, and some of the village maidens stood smiling shyly in the background. Before dismissing our Charikot coolies we had some important questions to ask the Rolwaling men. Would they be prepared to act as coolies for us, and could we get such items of food as rice, potatoes or tsampa? They promised the lot and we were overjoyed.

The Charikot men were anxious to be off and respectfully indicated to us that they would like to move down that very afternoon. This place was too cold for them in their thin and ragged clothing, and they felt they were amongst an alien people. So there was nothing for it but to set up the pay table and hand each man his twenty-seven rupees, with one rupee extra as baksheesh. For once we had met with coolies who took their wages and did not grumble. We shook each Nepali by the hand and felt a genuine sense of loss at goodbye, for these were the kind of men we remembered from Garhwal, simple unsophisticated souls with a natural gentleness of disposition that made them friends and companions, not mere servants. The Sherpas of Rolwaling were in the same distinguished class.

How wise the Charikot men were to get away we soon realised, for it became so cold that afternoon that we had to rake out our windproofs and woollen clothing to keep warm. The mists which had submerged the peaks all day had lowered to our level, and the air was as raw as on a winter afternoon in Scotland.

Summer, autumn and winter compressed into one day had left us such a feast of impressions that we crawled into our tents to try to digest them. It had been a wonderful march. When the mist cleared we would see what lay around us. It was like going to bed on Christmas Eve and wondering what would be in our stockings in the morning.

CHAPTER SIX

DISCOVERY—A HIDDEN MOUNTAIN RANGE

JAGGED ice peaks streaming with snow-spume encircled the camp when I looked out in the grey of the morning on a wan and wintry world spattered with new snow. There was no warm glow of sunrise on the high tops as I had hoped, but minute by minute the pale shapes of summits were being hung with silken garments in folds and flutings, with crinoline bulges where the bottle-green of glaciers was suspended over bare rock.

It was a long time before the sun climbed high enough over the gorge to warm the camp, and we watched with eagerness a searchlight advancing on us like a transforming ray, picking up grey rocks and autumn tints in a wave of colour that overspread us and changed the frosted grasses in an instant to diamonds. Red-billed choughs cackled like a tribe of merry jackdaws at the arrival of sudden warmth, and from the stream came a torrent of song in the wild notes of the whistling thrush. Like whirling snowflakes, the sun on their white wings, a flock of snow pigeons twisted and turned against the crags, hundreds of them in a joyful unison of motion.

The programme now was to get food and coolies in preparation for climbing and exploring in the upper regions beyond the haunts of man. We would assuredly get them, said the lamas, but not until tomorrow or the day after, for all the young men and women were either up in the mountains with their flocks of yaks and sheep or harvesting the potato crop before the onset of winter. Messengers had been sent out telling them to return, and when they arrived we would get all the help they could give. As far as we were concerned this arrangement was ideal. Douglas and George were anxious to go off with the gun and see what they could shoot, and Tom was keen to take photographs. I had some writing to do and wanted to look for birds in this high region. The Sherpas with much grumbling were sent six miles up the glen to make a depot of high-camp stores.

At this height of approximately 13,000 feet the bird life was of outstanding interest. Most birds of the Himalaya tend to have a vertical migration, in contrast to the more normal horizontal migration we are familiar with at home. By merely going uphill or downhill a Himalayan bird can change its season in an hour or two, making in that short time a change of food supply, habitat and temperature that in other lands can be normally achieved only by an immense flight across oceans or large land masses. One would naturally expect to find the high regions of the Himalaya almost denuded of bird life in the hard frosts of winter, but either the rhythm of migration is less definite among vertical migrants than among horizontal ones, or we saw a great many contradictions.

Here, for example, at an altitude of over 10,000 feet were three kinds of redstarts—white-capped, blue-fronted and plumbeous —in October still occupying their normal summer terrain. Amongst the scrub there were still plenty of tits and warblers, and a beautiful little orange-breasted hedge sparrow with red legs that sang with hurried song like our own British bird. There were babblers and thrushes, and quite a number of birds I could not identify, including some plain-looking mountain finches of a meally colour.

Tibetan ravens barked round the houses and lammergeier soared continually overhead. The latter is one of the biggest birds in the Himalaya, capable of adaptations to its structure that enable it to live at heights of over 27,000 feet above sea level. Though named as a vulture, it has the nobility of an eagle, and is in fact classified somewhere between the two. Even at close range it has none of the scrawny-necked and repulsive look of the griffon, which is the only other bird of the region to match it for size. Both are birds of the gorges rather than the foothills.

To watch the lammergeier soar on pointed wings, banking and gliding, each twist directed by the long and distinctively wedge-shaped tail, is to see absolute mastery of the air of the great mountains. One bird flew over to inspect me. The 'beard' or tuft of black feathers which gives it its other name of 'bearded vulture' hung down from under its chin and gave it a rather comical appearance. Its great head swung from side to side, its large eyes searching. At this close range it was possible to distinguish clearly the compressed bill and blunt short talons which mark it as a carrion-eater rather than a killer. An interesting peculiarity of the lammergeier is its fondness for the bones of animals, which it cracks open in much the same way as gulls crack mussels. It will pick up a large bone, fly with it to a height, and drop it at a suitable point to smash into splinters on the rocks below.

There were many birds I could not identify, including a yellow finch-like bird with black over the eyes. I expected to find rosefinches in great numbers in this alpine region but I saw only one, and it was an immature bird.

After lunch, when we had foregathered again in the tents, a lama invited us up to the pink house that was the 'gompa' or house of prayer. We all went up in a body, including the Sherpas, first to the chamber containing the prayer wheel, a ten-foot-high drum of giant girth covered with the gilt letters of Tibetan prayers and filled, we were told, with thousands of prayers written on slips of paper. Each man knelt in turn to the prayer wheel, kissed it, and in a series of ceremonial bows intoned prayers in a singing chant. Then the prayer wheel was sent spinning, a little bell sounding at each complete revolution. After each sahib had spun the drum we were allowed to enter the church proper.

In the semi-darkness of the interior the impassive face of a statue of Buddha glowed in the light of two butter lamps. Ceremony was important here, and each man prostrated himself several times, going forward at last to touch the altar with his head. At that point in the ceremony a lama hammered a great hanging drum, its hollow notes booming majestically in the confined space.

On either side of Buddha were alcoves or pigeon holes containing the holy prayer books, each wrapped in cloth and tabulated. Our eyes were drawn to a little boy who sat wearing a cardinal's cap and looking down on all this. He could not have been more than four years of age, but there was something almost majestic about him. There was dignity and refinement in his features, yet he never stopped smiling. His was the face of a saint. By his side sat a good-looking lama who was his guardian. The little boy was the reincarnation of a very holy lama, we were told, which meant that his was a very special place on earth. It was as if he knew he had a high mission in life to perform and was already ordained for it. We felt that the astrologers who had selected him knew their job. We were to see him round our camp often enough. The other little boys were mischievous, and like boys the world over were anxious to be noticed and larked with. But not the little lama. He took a keen interest in all that went on, smiling happily to himself with secret pleasure, but he made no attempt to talk or attract attention to himself.

Not wishing to offend prejudice or custom in the gompa we were very quiet and respectful, but it was soon evident that silence was not necessary once the formality of prayer was over. Everyone was laughing and talking, and in answer to the question whether we might take some pictures by flashlight, cymbals and long Tibetan horns were brought out, the latter emitting a sound more like a deep-throated animal roar than a musical instrument. One pretty female attendant posed in front of a wall fresco for us while we photographed its hell torments, graphically portrayed as a devil-fiend among the bodies of men and women in the grip of sin. The accent was on sex.

We were invited to a service next day, but little did we know what we were in for. Indeed it was such a fine morning that we were sorry we had accepted the invitation, and could hardly be persuaded to take our eyes from the viewfinders of our cameras, for the peaks were dazzlingly clear and the whole glen was filled with an intensity of colour. But we had to forego it and wend our way to the gompa, from which the clashing sounds of drums and trumpets had been coming since long before the first light. This was no ordinary affair. The purpose of the ceremony was to send the souls of recently departed dead in the right direction. Two of our Sherpas, Gylgen and Ela Tenzing, were footing the bill for it, and it cost them a hundred rupees each. Their mothers had died recently, and they regarded it as their duty to assist, so far as lay in their power, the journey of their parents to a higher life.

Little candles were burning and the library was being opened when we arrived. The books were about three times as thick as a volume of the *Encylopaedia Britannica*, but quite different in shape. They were composed of long narrow strips of hand-made paper, each about two feet long and six inches wide, printed in letterpress. The covers of the book were planks of wood. Each lama blessed his book ceremoniously before unwrapping it and removing the top plank. Then he began to chant the first prayer with fierce concentration. Soon a medley of chanting filled the room, growing in volume as more and more lamas arrived.

We were not left unattended. In front of us was a hollow tree-trunk filled with what looked like wet rice husks, and protruding from it were four bamboo sticks. We soon got the idea. The four sticks were straws, to be sucked. It looked a dubious proceeding and we whispered that we would pretend we were sucking. But it was obvious within a very few moments that no one was pretending. As the rice level went down our spirits went up, for the liquid that flowed through the bamboo was like good wine and twice as potent. Lamas and spectators were being plied with cups of it by female attendants, and if the noise in that confined place seemed overpowering it was because we did not yet know what real noise was.

Hour after hour the prayers went on. To the right of the statue of Buddha were the chief lamas, men of solemn face who prayed with fervour, turning over the leaves of their books at great speed. On the left were lesser figures who interrupted their prayers for laughter and talk. Sherpas we had never seen before came and went, fine-faced men clad in simple robes spun from natural wool and worn over baggy trousers clasped at the knee like knickerbockers and tucked into the tops of long woollen boots with yakskin soles. After bowing to Buddha and touching their heads on the floor before him they retired deferentially to the shadows. A bowl of rice grains was handed round so that we could take some for throwing over our shoulders at a given signal. We were glad when an interval was declared.

After the solemn gloom of the gompa the world seemed a brighter place, and slightly inebriated we tottered down the path to a little dell with a marvellous outlook. Its charm was that it had something of everything—the rich autumn colour of a Scottish glen, waterfalls and little alps like the best of Switzerland, and beyond, the spectacle of the Himalaya at its most dramatic. We looked towards a group of high and inaccessible peaks rising out of the rock walls of Rolwaling.

I had a lesson here on the necessity of sobriety and constant care in the Himalaya. Growing out of a clump of moss on a cliff was a cluster of gentians, their light blue contrasting with the glossy red of berries that grew alongside. I got my tripod out and was soon intent on the technical problem of capturing this on colour film, so much so that I forgot I was on a cliff, and stepped backwards to view the subject from another angle. But for Tom MacKinnon's leg I would have fallen. Luckily he had climbed down to watch me at work and I was able to grab him.

We got back to the gompa in time to witness the most moving part of the service. Gylgen and Tenzing now stood in front of the Buddha, one with a bowl of flame in his hand, the other with a bowl of corn from which rose tongues of flames. Enormous brass horns, reed pipes, hollow shells, cymbals and drums were upraised for action, and as we entered they burst forth in a fearful din.

It was not music but a rhythm of savage wildness bursting through the hoarse bellow of the horns and the thin bubblings of reed and shell. The cymbals clashed and syncopated to the accompaniment of a hollow drum beat, crashed louder and louder in a rush of tempo, swelled, faded, then rose again in a scalp-tingling noise as powerfully emotional as the discordant clashes and startling silences of a Honnegar symphony.

A busy service of chang kept musicians and lamas from going dry, and at length each man was given a little butter lamp to hold. We were nearing the crux of the ceremony, and Gylgen and Tenzing placed their candles on the table and prostrated themselves before the Buddha while a mighty solo of prayers from the head lama was intoned, interspersed with the ringing of a little hand bell as the style and tempo of the prayer changed.

The signal that the ceremony was over came when Gylgen went forward and paid a number of rupees to the treasurer. Then he offered chang to each lama in turn. He seemed to be overcome with emotion, as was Ela Tenzing. They were both in tears. I tried to sympathise with them, but when they answered by telling me it had cost them a hundred rupees each for all this, I had to be cautious in case they expected me to make a contribution.

After this we were invited up to the sanctuary of the head lama. He sat in a little recess like a cupboard, but it could not have been so very little for he was an enormous man, with a startling goitre that bulged on his neck like the rolls of a red scarf. His mouth hung open and there was something huge and friendly about his smile, revealing gaps in his great twisted teeth. Hanging out from under his cardinal's cap was a bushy fringe of black hair in contradiction to the wrinkles on his face. It was a yak's tail worn in the form of a wig. His body quivered when he laughed, and he laughed often.

We were plied with Tibetan tea and chang while he sat grinning in his alcove, which contained various treasured ornaments pertaining to the Buddha. To these treasures had been added our discarded flash bulbs of yesterday, the only Western note in this antique set-up. Quite shamelessly he asked us for baksheesh, and when we gave him some rupees asked for more.

'Om mani padmi hum, baksheesh?' I asked jokingly, and he laughed uproariously, his huge goitre shaking. 'Om mani padmi hum baksheesh,' he kept repeating. We were great friends by the time we left.

Nor had we seen the last of him, for he came with his beads next morning, not to see us off but to accompany us to where we were going. Everything had worked out as arranged. The

Sherpas were down from the hills and with them they had brought 398 pounds of native food in the shape of rice, beans, flour and tsampa. The men were a magnificently strapping lot, and Nyma was in his element, for these simple fellows sprang to obey his orders and he lorded it like a sahib. There were now so many of them about that we did not know which were coolies and which were followers. Everyone seemed to be carrying something except the head lama, who attached himself to me and asked me for more baksheesh. He got it too, and later I caught him gambling with it, playing dice beside a twenty-five-foot boulder carved from top to bottom with prayers.

To our surprise we saw some lamas following the mason's trade, carving out fresh prayers on suitable stones. They even had a scaffolding erected on one large boulder, and we were interested to see that they wore old Everest goggles to keep the granite chips out of their eyes. Their lives, it seemed, were dedicated to carving out prayers.

The explanation of the mass exodus from the village was forthcoming when we reached some little fields on the edge of a tangle of moraines. The villagers were going to gather potatoes at this cultivation area on the edge of the glaciers. There the clay provides soil and the stones have been cleared to make walls against the inroads of the yaks and sheep that graze under the incredible mountain face we came to call Rolwaling Wall. We could hardly have asked for a better base camp, for all round us were high and splendid mountains.

It was lucky we camped there, for hardly was the tent down when a three-quarters-dead Sherpa was brought to us. He had been caught out on a high pass in the bad weather a few days previously and was obviously in a bad way, unable to stand, with a racing pulse and pains in his head. When Tom tried to take his temperature he chewed the end of the thermometer and swallowed the bits. At the risk of losing our only other thermometer we found his temperature to be 104.5 degrees.

Tom sprang into action straight away with sulphanomide tablets and a demand for bedclothes. The man was carried to his draughty stone hut, placed on the earth floor and covered with woollen rugs. Two young children were snuggled in beside him as hot water bottles. We did not expect him to last until morning in the sharp cold of the Himalayan night, but either he was tougher than we thought or the M and B had done its work, for early next morning he was sitting up and grinning at us, giving us big salaams for saving his life. His temperature was down to normal, and though he still complained of pain in his bones we felt we could go off and climb without misgivings.

First we had to make a reconnaissance. The ideal peak for our purpose rose above us in two rock buttresses some 4,000 or 5,000 feet above our camp, at approximately 13,000 feet, and the approach by a ridge of pinnacles did not look easy. We were in high spirits, glad to be climbing at last in a world of silver and blue, for there was not a cloud in the sky and we could see every detail of snow and gleaming ice on the ice mountains surrounding us.

We started uphill with a will, but the steep 3,000 feet slog to the rocks took the stuffing out of us and brought home to us the fact that we were now climbing at heights greater than anything in the Alps. Moreover, the snow was soft and deep, and by the time we gained the rock crest of the summit ridge three of us were feeling the effects, with tight splitting headaches and feelings of sickness. But not Tom MacKinnon. As usual Tom was in grand form, for he has never suffered the effects of altitude.

I had been climbing with Tom and Dawa Tenzing and we had chosen a steep icy couloir. With a desperate effort I managed to keep up with them, until I felt a definite feeling of sickness stealing over me; then I unroped and told them to press on.

The other members of the party were 500 feet lower down and I waited for them, watching Tom and Dawa bounding off, climbing with élan on the steep rock rising to the sharp point of the summit. The gendarmes that had looked so difficult from below were turned one after another.

The others were not feeling so good but we had no intention of giving in, and a good thing too, for our headaches and sickness were forgotten as we came to life in some rock climbing on splendid granite—rough as the best in Glen Coe. The crux was a vertical thirty-foot crack defending the summit wedge, a delightful problem landing us on top. There was no sign of Tom. Not content with one peak he had pressed on to another linked by a high ridge. Soon we were jodelling to each other on our separate peaks and taking in as much of the view as we could, for bad weather was closing in fast.

We had climbed this peak to look into Tibet, to inspect if possible a group of mountains mentioned by Campbell Secord of Shipton's Cho Oyu party, but it was something quite different and unexpected that held our eyes. We were on the edge of a complex system of unmapped glaciers and ice and rock peaks on the south Rolwaling Gorge. This magnificent range was right on our doorstep, unsuspected but eminently approachable. The cartographers had obviously never gone behind the rock peaks we were on, hence the vagueness of the map. Shipton's party had been to the region on the north side of Rolwaling. It was going to be our privilege to be the first explorers of the south Rolwaling. If we could penetrate this system and climb some of its peaks we would be doing something of real exploratory value. The view was brief. Quite suddenly it was snowing and we were in mist, but we had seen what we wanted and now we headed down, much to Douglas's disgust, for he had hoped to emulate Tom and bring off a double by climbing the other rock peak.

It was as well we did not try it, for we found the descent trying, especially in the couloir. Also, we got a bit off-course in the mist and had difficulty in finding the route. Watching the slope ahead we hardly noticed that Douglas had fallen far behind and was stopping frequently to sit down. The effects of altitude are peculiar. George and I felt in good form on the descent until we got into camp, when both of us developed headaches and George was sick. Douglas came in looking pale and haggard. He took one mouthful of tea and was sick.

'Well, it was a fine climb anyway,' he said, disappearing inside his tent not to emerge again until next day.

While we lay on our lilo mattresses Tom skipped around, dosing us with gelusel and aspirin. The effect was such that inside an hour I felt lively and more than willing to tackle mutton soup, rice, vegetables, fried mutton and potatoes. Douglas and George were content with some Swiss beef tea. We had gone high rather too quickly and were paying the penalty.

Next day we were all up and about, eagerly discussing mountain plans for the exploration of the mountain group south of Rolwaling. Eight days' food, together with four tents for Sherpas and climbers, was about the maximum we could afford to carry into the area, considering the equipment of ropes, ice-claws, paraffin stoves, etc., necessary for the campaign.

While three of us organised food and equipment Tom was busy with his patient. The poor man had had a relapse, with a renewed pain in his side, and his temperature had jumped up to 104 degrees and more. We could not afford to stay and nurse him, for every day was a day into winter and a big snowstorm was forecast by the Sherpas. Certainly the weather looked as if it would change, with mackerel sky and a grey look of winter. This turned ominously to the first dramatic sunset of the trip, when the drifting clouds filling the Rolwaling became charged with a furnace glow and the ice curtain of Rolwaling Wall flared like a tongue of flame above them.

While Tom had been poulticing his patient for pneumonia with cloths filled with boiling flour, and injecting him with 1,000,000 units of penicillin, Nyma, our culinary expert, had produced a tin of gee (clarified butter) and two smelly hunks of yak meat.

I had feared we were to get that yak for dinner, and so we did, with a bonus of yellow yak soup as first course. The soup was little more than liquid grease, and the yak itself could be likened to a mixture of horse, beef and venison, except that it was considerably darker in colour, and might well have been mistaken for black puddings. Only Tom asked for a second helping, though Douglas was going strong until someone mentioned jaundice. This unfortunate reference put him off, and instead of asking for more he stopped eating entirely.

In the darkness of that night Tom was still busy with his patient. I held a torch for him while he put on yet another poultice. The head lama had been in to pray for the invalid and was to return shortly to sit up with him. The man was gasping as though with his last breath, and Tom hoped that the lama might be able to do by faith what he could not do with medicine. The hut was a mere hovel without rugs or any other comforts. A small fire burned in the centre of the earth floor, filling the room with smoke and outlining dimly the baskets of grain and potatoes and the cooking pots which were the only furnishings. Pathetically the woman bowed to us and offered us a basket of potatoes, which we refused.

We went to bed feeling that it was all over with the Sherpa, and felt sad, for he was a strong handsome man in the prime of his life and it looked as if Tom was in for his first failure as a doctor. Though he racked his brain for something else he might do he could think of nothing. Only time would tell.

CHAPTER SEVEN

THREE GOOD PEAKS

SKIES were grey and overcast that morning of 15th October when we left, in not very good temper, to establish our first high camp. We were wrathful because the Sherpas had refused to get up, while the Rowaling men who had been engaged to help in the upward carry stood around eagerly waiting for their loads. The last straw was when, in open defiance, Nyma began brewing up another basin of tea to keep us all waiting. I hurled it off the fire and told him to get moving. I also informed him that when we got to Namche he could consider himself fired.

This sort of unpleasantness, which we had never experienced with coolies before, was exasperating, particularly because it was all due to this one man. We should have fired him there and then and not allowed him to stay with our party. When eventually we did get rid of him there was a new feeling of gaiety among the Sherpas and ourselves, for although they were influenced by him they did not like him, as was obvious even during this dispute. Meanwhile the strong hand taken with Nyma did some good, and there was no further trouble for a time.

Tom was not with us when we moved off. He was anxious to see his patient and had been away from camp for some time. We climbed on a pleasant yak path, our coolies fairly rattling uphill despite their fifty-pound loads. The corrie we entered was a pleasant series of grassy alps, quite unlike the stony wilderness we had expected. There were even rude shelters

61

perched on a knoll, showing that in springtime this corrie was much used for the grazing of yaks and sheep. We climbed another thousand feet and came to the perfect camp site, a hollow containing a little lochan with half an acre of flat turf for the tents.

It was indeed an oasis, for everywhere around us was the sinister green of icefalls. We were curtained by ice, except on the north side, where Rolwaling plunged, rising on the other side to form the frontier ridge of Tibet. There row upon row of spectacular peaks make up the glaciated region entered for the first time by man in 1951, when Eric Shipton explored from a point west of Everest and discovered the col which gave him his view of Rolwaling. We were now looking on to that col.

When Tom joined us we were overjoyed to hear that his patient was still alive. Being almost as guarded in his opinion as a true member of the medical profession, he would not commit himself on the man's chance of pulling through. The matter was now out of his hands, and to take his mind off things we suggested that he should go off with George and make the most of the remaining daylight by reconnoitring the peak above.

Douglas and I stayed in camp to look at birds—to watch in particular two unusual birds of a type we had never seen before, about the size of snow buntings, and not unlike them in colour and musical twittering flight. What distinguished them was their red eyes and moustachial stripes. But for a prominent black eye-stripe their colour was like the winter plumage of the snow bunting, and my own belief is that they were some type of bunting, though it is possible they were of the shorelark family.[1] It was a surprise to find blue-fronted and white-capped redstarts, for this is the limit of their summer range. Dashing hither and

[1] Dark bill, dark legs, size about that of a sparrow, dark band on tail, light crown, striated back, light cheeks, buff area on flanks. Flight pattern black and white.

thither over our tents was a falcon the shape of a peregrine and about the same size, but of a pale brown colour.

Despite a Scotch mist that had crept down early in the afternoon Tom and George had managed a fine reconnaissance. They had been up to 18,000 feet and had seen a likely route on a superb peak we had admired from afar but on which we had scarcely hoped to find a route, accustomed as we were to Himalayan peaks turning out to be much steeper than they look. But Tom and George were optimistic, and so full of confidence in their route under the west precipice of the peak that our spirits went up with theirs.

At 17,000 feet they had seen a wading bird with a curved bill like a curlew's which flew past with shrill calls. Undoubtedly this was an ibis bill, on migration from Tibet perhaps, where they commonly nest. We were to see quite a number of them throughout the trip.

Talking, speculating on the weather as night drew round us, we were suddenly aware of a weird red light glowing through the mist, unfolding before us spectral ice curtains with the glow of firelight playing on their crests, so enormously high above the trembling and heaving clouds that we could not believe in them at first. Soon they were hidden again as the grey sea filling Rolwaling boiled over us.

Whatever misgivings we may have felt that night about weather vanished later when we crawled outside the tent to look on stars that sparkled with frost and a sky that quivered with electric brilliance as though from the Northern Lights. Every cloud had been vanquished, and although there was no moon the peaks stood out as if cut out of the cardboard of some fantastic stage setting. The stillness in that frozen world was absolute until an ice avalanche shook the night and warned us that it was time for sleep, if we were to be up with the dawn to find a way through the maze of ice ahead.

One of the triumphs of human nature is its capacity for transforming discomfort into living adventure. That is the way of mountaineering. We tend to remember the good things, the important things, the things which have roused us to a peak of living, such as a rock or ice problem successfully solved, or an arresting view that fills the heart and mind with waves of pleasure and lasting satisfaction. The other details, such as the business of getting up in the morning, cooking, struggling with frozen boots, sinking into deep snow, slipping about on icy boulders or toiling up interminable moraines, the effort of climbing when every muscle of one's body cries for a rest and unacclimatised breath comes in gasps as if each mouthful of rarified air is the last—these things slip away into the limbo of things forgotten.

What I shall remember to the end of my days is the thrill of camping on an ice-ridge at 19,000 feet, just below the summit of our peak, when a grey mist surrounding us took on the hue of fire. As we hastily dragged on boots and stepped outside the sun burst on a smouldering world, flaming on peaks and jagged edges that leapt out of a chaos of smoke. We might have been witnessing the birth of the earth as pinnacles black and gigantic were swallowed up and released one after another in a turmoil of fiery vapour.

We had never before beheld such a scene or felt so little part of the universe—three tents in the clouds with a window into the most savage mountains and the deepest ravines on earth. We looked across a cloud sea of fire stretching across the breadth of Nepal to India. Only the dark whale-backs of ridges projected out of its ruffling waves. Over the zenith was spreading a wash of green paling to yellow in contrast to the flaming landscape of earth. We were receiving at that moment the greatest reward that mountaineering has ever given us. Yet shortly before this sight I felt so ill that for the first time on the expedition I was unable to write my diary.

Getting to this position had been harder than the reconnaissance report led us to expect.   Out of six Sherpas two fell ill and proved useless for climbing.   Their loss put a strain on the remainder and on us.   Tom, as our strongest and fittest man, broke a trail through the snow, an exhausting and knee-deep job.

The climb from the moraine to the glacier, which had looked easy, proved trying because of the new snow lying on boulders and filling the hollows.   We tried to keep on the boulders, using their uneven spacing rather than sink deep at each step. Inevitably such jerky progress broke the rhythm of breathing so essential to comfortable climbing on mountains, reducing us to impotence in the heat of the sun and the dullness of glacier lassitude.

We had hoped to go direct from 16,000 to 19,000 feet, but in the deep snow it was an over-ambitious programme.   The four Sherpas, Nyma, Mingma, Ela Tenzing and Dawa Tenzing, were magnificent here.   For the first time we were seeing them at their splendid best.   They climbed with a will and made no bones about carrying the kit.   This was their territory and they were proud to be better than other men.

Tom with his usual energy and optimism took a straight line up the glacier, but even with a trail flogged for them the Sherpas could not follow him, and they beat their own in a series of zigzags.   Douglas, George and I were not feeling so good here, and luckily neither were the Sherpas.   They were tiring, and they laid down their loads to beat out the trail before carrying them up.   This splendid plan gave us respite, and as it turned out meant no more climbing for us that day, for it was almost sunset by the time they returned to their luggage.   But they had flogged a trail to the point which we had earmarked as destination, and happily we all descended to clear a place for camp, a place where we could listen all night to the squeaking of the glacier as it moved along its bed.

There was frost inside as well as outside the tent next morning, when we looked on peaks sharp as knives and flushed with the rosy glow of dawn.   The time was a quarter to six and we lit the stoves and got the kettles on before calling the porters to share a communal breakfast of tsampa, biscuits, cheese and tea.   It was noticeable that the sahibs forced it down while the Sherpas ate with pleasure.   We felt glad to be alive and thankful to be nowhere else on earth but on this particular place.

In the crispness of that invigorating morning we could move fast, for the trail broken yesterday was now a frozen path and we made good time up it, such good time that at nine o'clock we reached the little col which had been our objective on the previous day.

We were on a lip above a wild chaos of glacier and icefall flowing southward in a dazzle of séracs and contortions of ice. Three peaks formed its head like studs in a horseshoe.   Nearest to us was the sharp rock peak we hoped to climb.   Across the dipping welter of ice were the other two peaks, higher and icier than anything else in the wild mountain scene.   We were, in short, in a key position not for one peak but for three.   The problem was, would any of them be climbable?

As it was only nine o'clock and the Sherpas were still far behind, we sat down to take stock of our position.   On every side was the glitter of ice slopes reaching up to shining crests on a sky so dark blue as to appear almost black.   The peak we had come to climb looked more reasonable now that we were close to it, but we were not counting our chickens, for there were still 1,000 feet of steep glacier heavily seamed with crevasses to climb before we could set foot on the south ridge by which we hoped to reach the summit.   As this was likely to take us time to test and make safe, we sent down Ang Dawa and Mingma, who expressed their willingness to return to camp 2 and fetch up the loads left by the sick Sherpas.   They showed us their mettle that day and we gained a new respect for them which was heightened in the next few days.

The slope ahead was purgatorial, both in its steepness and in its depth of new snow, particularly as the sun was torturing us with heat and glare. We plunged to the knee at each step, and for the first time in my life I vomited on a mountain. What I was suffering from was dehydration, caused by an insufficiency of liquid to combat the effects of sweating. The going was so slow that the Sherpas had returned to Camp 2 and regained the col before we reached the top of that heartbreaking slope.

We waited at the crevassed section and fixed ropes so that we could take over the loads from the Sherpas and allow them to return to the col for another load. Douglas and Tom did the bulk of the carrying here. This climb with loads gave us some idea of what the Sherpas accomplished that day in relaying six loads amongst four men. At 19,000 feet that night we had two tents for the four of us and one Sherpa.

It was while we lay in the tents as if in some death coma, with mist swirling round us, that we became aware of the fiery glow which heralded the clearing which I have already described. This clearing of the clouds also gave us the first sight of that south ridge of our mountain on which we had staked our chances. Bathed in orange light a slender rock tower was set above a blade of snow which dropped at a gentle angle. The only obstacle between us and it was an ice wall—very steep it is true, but it looked incapable of stopping us. If the final tower was of sound rock, and the weather held, we would certainly get to the top tomorrow. We judged the summit to be little more than 1,000 feet above us. If I had any worry it was that I might not manage to summon up enough strength to climb it.

As the amber clouds paled and the darkness of the night came down we felt the bite of the cold. On the horizon where lay the Indian plains there was now only a dull smoulder, paling to a band of yellow which spread in an opalescent wave over the whole sky. It took us an hour or two to get warm, even wearing all our clothes in our sleeping bags, but we could not help looking out from time to time to see the stars, near and brilliant, shining above these Himalayan peaks. Our breath froze on the tent canvas, yet a few hours before we had been complaining of the glare of the sun and its fierce dehydrating heat.

We waited to feel something of this heat before getting up in the morning, though there was not a breath of wind and hardly a cloud except for hog backs of cumulus lying on the foothills far below. We melted snow for a breakfast of dried eggs and biscuits, cheese, marmalade and tea, and set out for our peak as the tent started to run wet from the melting armour of ice inside and out. We roped up, and walked easily on crisp, gently rising snow to a bergschrund formed where the glacier had pulled away from the steep ice wall barring access to the ridge. Tom was in his element at the prospect of a difficult problem, and was soon showing us he could whack out steps here with the same vigour as on an Alpine peak. For the first time we saw Dawa and Mingma and Dawa Tenzing on a place demanding real knowledge of snow and ice technique, and we were amazed at their proficiency. They moved like Swiss guides and were anxious to take over the lead from Tom.

But Tom was not having any. The responsibility of the place was his, and in 200 feet of steep cutting he was up and over the bulging cornice and on the crest of the ridge. Up after him went the Sherpas, who were so keen to get to the top that they all but hoisted us up the wall, myself remonstrating angrily between sharp gasps of breath as I tried to keep pace with the pull of the rope.

The ridge before us stretched broadly ahead, snow-corniced and overhanging on one side and falling gently away on the other.   We followed its crisp surface filled with the anticipation of a good rock climb on a turret of red-grey rock which sprang in one sweep from snow to summit.   The rock was magnificent, almost like gabbro, and its rough surface was well provided with sound holds until the last step, where it became smoother in a final taper to a point with room on top for only three men. Here was perfection, salt to the egg, in a last little rock problem.

Life was at its best for us then.   Here we were on the summit and the day was young enough to enable us to enjoy it without feeling anxiety about the way down.   For the first time in our Himalayan experience we were having the reward of a wide view from a summit.   In Garhwal in 1950 we had climbed continually in cloud, and always there had been anxiety about the way down.   We could now sit in the sunshine at leisure and more than make up for these disappointments as we surveyed a sweep of mountains stretching north, south, east and west. The 'treasurehouse stored up for a future generation of explorers' was all ours.

Grey Rolwaling seemed impossibly far down, yet only a hop across it was Tibet, so clear that we looked far beyond the frontier into range upon range of massive ice peaks.   Only Eric Shipton and his party have touched their fringe.   Due east was Sola Khombu, its peaks mostly hidden by near masses of rock and ice, solid and formidable mountains where the map showed nothing but vague sketches; not minor peaks but mountains with raw and jagged ridges and glaciers that hung like wallpaper to their sides.

From where we were sitting we could now judge our chances of climbing one or the other of the two ice peaks forming the horseshoe round the glacier head.   By our climbing of this peak we had unlocked the gateway to them, for we looked down on the one chink in their armour of icefall and crevasse.

From here we could see the ridge of our peak swing round to meet a large and unbroken snowfield sweeping up in a plateau of 20,000 feet. Out of this plateau rose the higher of the two peaks, a snow dome bulging with cornices in a rise of some 22,000 feet. We would never have a better chance of a high Himalayan peak, that was obvious. The more we studied it the better the prospect appeared. The depth of the new snow and the possibility of an avalanche on the steep slopes leading to the summit were the only doubtful factors.

We asked the Sherpas their opinion and they nodded emphatically. They thought the peak climbable and urged us to try it. At the same time they pointed to the sky and said that we were in for bad weather and would need to be quick. Tom was all eagerness to get down and start for the peak that very afternoon. We could leave a rope on the ice wall and come back up in our own steps, so that the only trail-breaking would be the trek across the plateau. With luck we might get the peak tomorrow.

There was only one fly in the ointment, and that was Sherpas. At best we had only four capable of doing any hard work, and of these four only two could be absolutely relied upon. Further, if the weather was going to break and speed was necessary it introduced the factor of acclimatisation, and of our own party only Tom was thoroughly acclimatised and a rival in speed to the Sherpas Mingma and Dawa Tenzing. If lightness and speed were the essentials, then Tom alone should make the bid for the summit. With only one stove, one tent and their own personal kit they would not be overburdened.

Tom, who is a modest man, had to be persuaded that he was the one for the attempt. Nor would he go until he had written out a chitty accepting responsibility for the deaths of the Sherpas if such a thing should occur.

We stormed down the tower, swung down the fixed rope on the ice wall and were soon in camp, bundling gear together and mak-

Sola Khombu — the road to Everest.

Sherpas and sahibs: Front row L. to R. George Roger, Tom Weir, Douglas Scott and Tom McKinnon. Dawa Tenzing: second left back row.

Sprawling Katmandu.

The silver doorway of the temple of Machendranath.

The peculiarly Chinese style of Newar architecture is reflected in elegant pagodas, rich red brickwork, and superb wood carving.

Man hauling a motor car over the pass to Katmandu.

Himalayan taxi service.

Natural vegetation has been cut away to make rice and wheat terraces. Soil erosion signs are common everywhere in Nepal.

Variety is the true delight of Himalayan travel.

L. to R.: Tom Weir, Tom McKinnon, George Roger and Douglas Scott.

Suspension bridge across the Sun Kosi river.

A Taman coolie shows the sharpness of his kukri by shaving the hairs of his legs with its keen blade.

High on a hilltop a Nepali woman spreads her corn to dry.

An itinerant musician strums a tune while his small boy dances.

After the monsoon damp the corn is spread to dry.

The labour of thousands of years has gone into the terracing of these vast hillsides.

Nepali hill dwellers stack their Indian corn, and suspend the heads ready for use round the walls. The long vegetables are pumpkins, and above them is a tray of spices.

Wayside shrines with ledges for coolies to rest their loads occur every few hundred yards on the main routes.

Crossing the Rolwaling Khola.

Undergrowth in the Rolwaling Gorge.

Bhotias of the upper Bhote Kosi.

In the heart of the Rolwaling Gorge — Gauri Sanker above.

The cheerful people of Beding find everything a joke.

The little lama of Beding village with his guardian.

A cheery man, the head lama of Beding, whose goitre did not prevent him climbing to the base camp with us. The fine head of black hair is a yak's tail.

Prayers begin with loud bangs on the drum that hangs from the roof of Beding Gompa. Round the walls of the temple are bright paintings from Tibet.

The first 20,000ft. peak was climbed from the glacier on the right.

Eyrie camp on first Rolwaling peak.

Approaching the summit of our first 20,000ft. peak.

The summit, with room only for three men.

Tom McKinnon looks at the snow dome peak on the left and reckons it will go.

Above Rolwaling — Tibet border peaks rise beyond.

Steep rock on first rise of Tesi Lapcha.

Traversing to the glacier for the final climb.

The way continues up the rock face on the left to outflank the ice.

From the glacier the route is over the gap for descent of Tesi Lapcha for Sola Khombu.

One Beding Sherpa carries an 80lb. load of firewood and the other a 70lb. crate.

These Sherpanis never lost their happy smiles despite the hardships of a particularly arduous route.

From Thyangboche looking to Tesi Lapcha — far right.

Crest of the Tesi Lapcha Pass. Descent to Sola Khombu.

The nimble fingered Gurkha made a basket in less than two hours.

A lesson in writing Tibetan brings furrows to the brows of Namche children. We saw no girls in the school.

The girl wants to know if she can come with us as a porter.

Camp at Periche grazing-ground close to the Khombu glacier which drains from Everest.

The ice world of Sola Khombu from the summit of our modest rock peak.

Gorges on the Dudh Kosi below the Mount Everest Massif. Amadablam on the right.

The Khombu Glacier and Everest, whose summit appears over the rock curtains of Nupse.

A young lama of Thyangboche Monastery stands by the prayer wall which stretches for quarter of a mile, each stone bearing a prayer.

Amadablam from Kumjung village.

The track to Everest, by jungle ridge and bare mountain walls. Everest is the first ice peak on the left. The tower on the right is Amadablam.

A dangerous bridge across the Dudh Kosi which caused much prayer from the porters as they went over.

The village of Beding in the heart of the Rolwaling Gorge.

ing up the food for the attempt. By early afternoon they were ready to go. We said our farewells and watched them fairly shoot up the ridge. Our thoughts were with them as we crawled into the tents with headaches which we blamed on the fierce sun.

Perhaps if we had stayed in that camp another night we would have attempted the peak ourselves. As it was, we were visited that afternoon by three Sherpas, one of the sick men having recovered. They complained of the cold in their snow camp and urged us to go down to a little moraine island some 1,500 feet below. Douglas, whose ideals take no account of physical discomfort, was depressed at such a prospect. His inclination was to advance on the peak and try to follow Tom, but he sportingly acknowledged that he was not feeling well enough for it, nor were the porters properly equipped for cold camps on snow.

Down there, as the night flushed the peaks with pink, we wondered how Tom and his Sherpas were faring in their little tent perched somewhere on that great expanse of virgin glacier. If we knew him, he would be tingling with excitement, and settled in his sleeping bag by now, replete with a big meal. He would sleep like a log too. The weather looked settled and the frost that night was keener than usual, making us snuggle into our sleeping bags immediately the sun set.

Dawn broke on the perfection of a day for mountaineering, clear, crisp, with no threatening cloud in the sky. For us it was a climb down over glacier and moraine to reach our turfy corrie, with its little loch which we saw with new delight. Three redstarts sat as if awaiting us, the white-capped, blue-fronted and, rather amazingly, the plumbeous, at the greatest height I have ever seen it in summer or winter. Huge loads of firewood had been brought up by the coolies and in no time we had fires going for a great feast of potatoes, rice, lentils, etc., for we had only picked at our food on the heights.

71

At half-past two we were leaning back, chatting, with that meal tight against our waist belts, when we heard a shout from above. It was Tom. What had gone wrong, we wondered? It was inconceivable that he had climbed the peak, for it was just twenty-five hours since he had left us. But he *had* climbed it, and Dawa and Mingma were beaming all over, as happy as schoolchildren. At 9.15 that morning they had been on the summit around 22,000 feet. Now at 2.20 they were in camp at 16,000 feet and apparently as fit as fleas.

Bit by bit we heard the story. Breaking the trail to establish a camp at 20,000 feet had been tough, owing to a rapid deterioration in the snow caused by the heat of the afternoon sun. At sunset the two porters and Tom had piled into the little mountain tent and brewed pemmican soup, reinforced with tsampa, which was followed by biscuits and jam. Despite the cold, which he described as severe, they slept well and made an early start, though they were delayed a little as a fine powdery snow had been blown into the tent by the wind, and buried everything.

They were on their way at seven o'clock and had to move fast to keep warm. The snow was good though not uniform, and they broke through deeply in places. At other places they rattled up, step-kicking on secure slopes but occasionally traversing below cornices ripe to release avalanches. The route was always obvious, he said, for it followed the line of least resistance, zigzagging on the steep slopes. Dawa and Mingma were in their element, and each took a turn at leading. They never halted and could hardly believe it when suddenly there were no more slopes to climb and they were on the summit, looking across to Everest and Cho Oyu, recognised and saluted instantly by Dawa, who had climbed with Shipton on both of these peaks.

It was uncomfortably cold for standing around but the moment was not one to be lost by hurrying down. The peak stood above a tangle of ravines plunging south, and Tom reckoned he

72

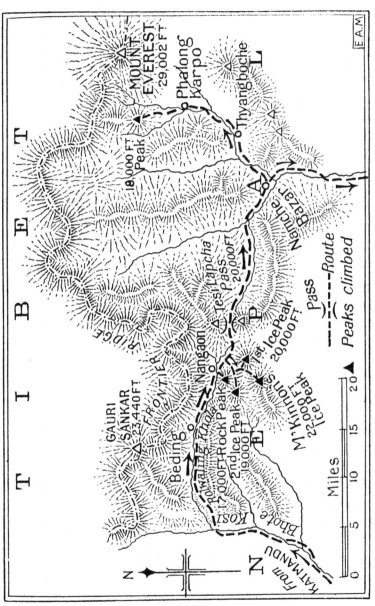

Rolwaling and the Tesi Lapcha.

could have made a new pass across the range from the Rolwaling to the Likhu Khola, a consideration that weighed with him in the event of bad weather preventing their return by the way they had come. He had closely inspected the high ice wall connecting his snow dome to the third peak of our trinity but had seen no route that made him keen to try it. Everywhere to the north and east were the jagged peaks which hem the country of Sola Khombu.

Ten minutes on top and they began the descent, which, as on all steep ice peaks, demanded more care than the climb. The two Sherpas, though over forty years of age, were like school-boys, he said, and rolled over in the snow in delight, kicking their legs and laughing heartily, pointing gleefully to the peak from time to time. Back in camp they wasted not a moment, and thanks to their well-made trail were able to traverse glacier and ice wall without the need for route-finding. We were proud to be associated with such a brilliant piece of sound and energetic mountaineering. In another corner of the camp Dawa and Mingma were describing their part of the ascent, and judging by the amount of waving and pointing that was going on, it was losing nothing the telling.

Now we had something to point out to Tom. That day as we descended to this camp we had speculated to some effect on the possibility of climbing a shapely rock point that rose out of a glacier to the west of us in a steep and continuous edge promising 2,000 feet of rock climbing at least. If the rock was as good as the rock we had climbed on to date, we were offered an outstanding climb. We judged the peak to be about 19,000 feet or over, and our intention was to try it in one day from our present camp, for it was not far away.

We wanted Tom's opinion and advice, for we intended to go at it next day. Naturally we did not expect him to come with us, for we thought he would need a rest.

74

'Rest?' he said. 'Rest when you are dead. I'm coming right with you!' And so he did.

The ground was still white with frost when we set off after the sharpest cold that three of us had ever felt in the Himalaya, though Tom had been colder in his high camp the night before. Astonishingly, the Sherpas, whom we had cursed all through the expedition because they would not get up in the mornings, were up before dawn, with boiling water ready for us.

A little tsampa and egg sufficed for breakfast, and we got away by half-past seven, moving fast to keep warm. We literally raced to meet the sun, and whenever we felt its rays warm us we sat down to enjoy our position overlooking the little corrie by the tarn, now frozen over. At this height of 17,000 feet we found dwarf blue poppies whose seeds rattled inside faded petals like crinkled paper. As it was a type of poppy we had never seen before, Tom collected the seeds in the little cellophane bags he carried specially, so that he could label each specimen as he found it and later pass it to Kew. By moraine and crevassed glacier we contoured under the north face of our peak, heading for the one obvious breach in the face which offered access to our chosen ridge. We moved fast now to avoid stonefall danger, and roped for the crevassed section and the crossing of the bergschrund.

We climbed in three parties, Douglas with Ang Dawa, Tom with Kamin, and I with George and Nyma. There was a holiday feeling abroad, for none of us was laden with heavy kit. One hundred feet of steep and icy rocks and we were out of the shadow of the north face into the sunshine of the east ridge. The rock was, as we had hoped, of sound reddish granite shattered into pinnacles crushed into masses of huge boulders in places, with inviting cracks and chinks in the walls. The scale was so vast that we felt fortunate to have previous knowledge of a likely route, for we had picked out a landmark in a tall tower and knew we should pass close to it, on the left of where it rose above us now.

Douglas, who is a superb rock climber, started up a direct route but was forced back into an easier line. Our party followed Tom, who was already weaving a way round corners and up slabs and vertical chimneys, finding delight in every situation, particularly where the crag fell sheer away on its south side for thousands of feet. We climbed a long slab above this drop—not easy, but not so difficult as to interfere with complete enjoyment of the situation. Like all great climbs this one seemed to go on and on, giving us so much of interest that we were scarcely aware of the altitude.

We were now on the south wall of the mountain rather than on the ridge. We climbed in grooves which suddenly sheered to a perfect point, with room for only one at a time on its top. Loud jodels and cries of pleasure filled the air as the first man took his stance on the summit. For enjoyment this had been a climb as good as any in the Alps, and for good measure the last move on to the summit was quite awkward. The time was only 12.30, so a big slice of the day still remained.

Poised on the top we looked between our feet to the Rolwaling Khola some 8,000 feet below, its path a thread on the south wall of Gauri Sankar. At this height the trees and autumn-brilliant shrubs which had so charmed us by their rich colour were flattened out into a general impression of dark austere slopes. The hugeness of the landscape spread before us would have given an overpowering impression of barrenness but for the certain knowledge of the little things that make up so much of the joy of Himalayan travel, the feasts of colour lying round every corner, the camping places among alps gay with flowers.

Up here we had the best of two worlds because we could read into the scene spread before us. For example, we could see through binoculars our footsteps zigzagging in a long trail over glacier to our camp of two nights ago at 19,000 feet, but—more exciting—we could pick out a trail above that weaving in and out amongst the ice cliffs of Tom's peak to end on the summit. That was one world—a world of action and adventure and nights in high camps—that we would remember to the end of our lives.

Then there was the other world of Rolwaling, the forest of dead trees we had traversed, now only one of many great bluffs of hillside dropping to the grey snake of the river which we could see wriggling down its turbulent course, dropping thousands of feet out of a paradise of autumn colour to jungle green and bamboo where flies and leeches had bitten. The whole mighty scene was ours.

This was our last peak in Rolwaling. We had climbed four mountains in the last eight days and now it was time to descend. Getting off a big rock peak is invariably more difficult than getting on—not in terms of technical difficulty so much as in route-finding—and this peak was no exception. The exposure of the climb gets rubbed home too, especially if a stone should fall and show what would happen to a body should it become suddenly detached. We saw enough on that downward climb to make us take great care. It was a surprise to discover too how much we had zigzagged from the south wall to the ridge and back again.

We foregathered above the schrund and roped up in threes for the passage of the glacier, then plunged down to join the moraine. Soon each man was jogging his own course home, some down to the tarn to walk round it, some over another little top above the camp. The afternoon clouds had formed by the time we got down to camp and Rolwaling was submerged, the vapours rising up from time to time in towers that caught the fire of an exceptional sunset flaming on the peaks. The meal which we had been looking forward to was forgotten as cameras clicked, trying to capture the extraordinary sight of brilliant orange peaks rising out of fiery tongues of cloud.

That night we had a discussion on what we should do next. There was no shortage of peaks for climbing if we concentrated on bagging them. Alternatively we might consider a complete change of scene by organising a crossing to the Nangpa La region, or Everest by way of the Tesi Lapcha, which had been crossed by Hillary from east to west less than twelve months before at the end of the Everest reconnaissance. No mountaineer had crossed the pass from our side, and his description of it as a very difficult pass rather intrigued us, for it crosses the main range at nearly 20,000 feet. Indeed we had seen where it went across and had been considerably impressed by the place. From it we could descend into the legendary district of Sola Khombu, not only among the greatest peaks in the world but into the home country of the Sherpas. It was an alluring prospect.

A deciding factor was the constant reiteration of the local men that we were shortly to have a big snowstorm. The threat had been hanging over us for a week and we could not altogether discount it. As the Tesi Lapcha would take several days to cross and would be impossible after a snowstorm had drifted it up, it seemed a question of now or never.

We decided on 'now,' and retired to bed for one of the best sleeps of the expedition, from nine o'clock until eight the next morning. In the clear air of this fine mountain shelf it seemed sacrilege to go down, but the decision had been made and if we were a little reluctant the porters were jubilant.

Not a villager remained in Nangaon when we got down to it, and the Sherpas took advantage of their absence to commandeer a hut and smooth out the yak dung in front of it for our tents. Much to their disgust we refused to camp on it, and with drawn brows they carried all our goods to the river several hundred yards away.

All we wanted them to do was go down to the gompa some six miles away and ask the head lama to send us up sixteen porters and 160 pounds of firewood. If we got the porters we could cross the pass, starting off on the day after tomorrow. If we did not, then we would climb some more peaks in this region. We waited until next day, impatient not only to hear our prospects but also to get news of the sick Sherpa.

CHAPTER EIGHT

MOUNTAIN CROSSING—THE TESI LAPCHA

THE providence that looks after drunk men, babies and mountaineers must have been with us when thirteen men and five women were despatched up to us, not next day but on the morning scheduled for the attempt on the pass. But what overjoyed us even more was the news that the sick man doctored and poulticed by Tom was restored to health. The most surprised man was Tom himself, whose only comment was, 'Well, it just shows how tough these Sherpas are!'

How tough these Rolwaling Sherpas were we later discovered; indeed they were not ordinary men and women but of the stuff of which heroes are made. Little did we know as we looked them over in their baggy homespuns and Tibetan boots that they were rock climbers of whom any mountaineering club might be proud—except that no member of any mountaineering club known to me could do what they did. They lost their shyness but never their grins, despite a hard and uncomfortable route. Three of the women were Tibetan beauties, very small, round-faced, slant-eyed and red-cheeked, and the men vied with each other for their smiles.

Also with us was a young lama from the gompa at Beding who was going to Thami and afterwards through to the Rongbuk Monastery on the north side of Mount Everest. The chance to join our caravan going over the Tesi Lapcha was too good to miss apparently, the only other route to Khombu being a tedious detour round the range. He told us of passes across the range which only lamas have crossed, and very holy lamas at that, so we felt he was an acquisition to the party, even though he came as a tourist rather than as a porter.

The first march was a short one, to an oasis situated above a glacial desert of rubble, borne down by a huge ice stream, that filled the centre of a whole cirque of peaks. We would find no water and no camping place if we went on, they said, which we thought was a bit steep as the time was only one o'clock and we were paying them the cash equivalent of 6/9 a day.

We judged our height to be about 15,000 feet, and could see nothing of the Rolwaling Gorge but the rocky tops of the peaks above it. Long grey moraines projected on each side of us in a chaos of boulders up which we had zigzagged to reach this mainstream of ice.

This oasis was all the more delightful when we took stock of our surroundings, so boulder-strewn that there was nowhere to walk except on top of the stone piles cast up by the glaciers. Debris as though from an earthquake or atomic explosion stretched as far as the eye could see, to a Kanchenjunga-like face of ice blocking the whole head of the valley. Cradled in this boulder desert was a fair-sized lake, a grey sheet of water with bits of ice floating in it. The crash and rumble of falling stones sounded continually from its high and unstable banks.

Opening out from the main ice stream were several side streams, subsidiary glaciers leading up to ice peaks we recognised as having seen on our climbs. Many looked feasible from this side, especially a ridge of pinnacles like a gigantic Cuillin of Skye at a height of about 19,000 feet. Immediately over our camp was an ice peak so fluted and ice-pinnacled that we wondered how its narrow corniced ridge could support it. Near here we saw the footprints of a wolf.

The Rolwaling Sherpas knew how to make themselves comfortable. Some were rock climbing in bare feet, searching for juniper on the cliff face, while others were cooking in little syndicates of two and three, each with its own fire. Over one fire we could make out a head wearing a fine eiderdown bala-clava helmet. It was 'Chomolungma baksheesh,' its owner having been given it in 1933 when he was on Everest with Ruttledge. This rather fine-featured Sherpa showed us a chitty stating that he had gone to Camp 4 at 24,000 feet on Everest but had broken down on the way to Camp 5. After that he had been seconded to Spender to assist in the photo survey. With him at his fire was his wife. The unattached women kept their own fire, but they were seldom without visitors and the Sherpas laughed knowingly when we appeared on the scene.

The new moon was riding on a clear sky and the peaks stood in silhouette when we went over to present some tea and sugar to the Rolwaling men, who were now installed in caves, singing and laughing, completely happy in each other's society and taking no notice of the cold. They had fuel, food and shelter, so the long night held no terrors for them. With cheery grins they bade us goodnight, and as we snuggled into our eiderdown bags we wondered how we would fare if all we had to keep us warm was homespuns and a fire in a cave.

The loch was frozen hard in the morning but the Sherpas were already up and cooking when we rose, and in a remarkably short time we were on our way, following an astonishing route.

First the way lay on the narrow edge of a moraine, which soon broadened to a boulder-field of loose stones many miles long. We climbed up or went down according to which looked easier, but the going was never really easy. Always there was the rattle of stonefall, sometimes from the steep slopes below us but more often from the wall above, which sent down boulders released from their bed of boulder-clay to whizz through the air and land in the trough at our feet. Without this trough of moraine separating us from the cliff we should have been in mortal danger. As it was, we always expected something to bound clear over the trough. The Sherpas had no such fear. They tiptoed from stone to stone, hardly bothering to glance at the face above.

There was one rather terrifying part of the route where a side glacier held a mass of huge boulders in temporary suspension. It was a tottering wall kept in position only by clay. Despite the obvious danger we could not get the coolies to make a detour. They preferred walking under this artillery to stumbling into the midstream chaos of the glacier. It certainly was a 'kharab rasta' (an unpleasant route), but how these Rolwaling Sherpas could carry!

We were close under the great ice wall and wondering where next when the leading Sherpas proposed a halt. It was a good suggestion because the party was much too strung out. While we waited the Sherpas found running water and opened up their rations of tsampa to make a quick gruel. We added glucose to ours, but even by itself tsampa is a life-giving food. It is the ideal iron ration for travelling in an arid country like this because it can be eaten raw. It is wheat or barley which has been roasted and ground, and though it seems rather coarse and tasteless at first, one quickly gets used to it. The Sherpa likes it best stirred into hot water or tea until it is dark brown and thick as dough, accompanied by side dishes of rice and lentils strongly flavoured with spices. Breaking off a lump of tsampa they scoop up some rice and lentils, and pop the lot into their mouths. A Sherpa normally eats about two pounds of food a day.

Once we had all foregathered, rested and eaten, we swung up away from the glacier, to outflank the considerable icefall blocking our path. We climbed now on a cone of avalanche debris but were soon forced on to the main wall of a rock peak, traversing a ledge where the holds were earthy and we were exposed to a considerable drop. It was balance climbing, and we watched with amazement men and women move carefully from one foothold to another, as confidently as ourselves despite their awkwardly suspended loads which enforced a difficult stiff-necked position.

Like all hill people the Rolwaling men and women use headbands for supporting the weight of their loads. This is the ideal way of carrying a burden on dangerously steep slopes. Instead of shoulder straps a special rope with a broad band for the head is adjusted round the baggage at the point of balance. If danger threatens a Sherpa need only throw back his head to get rid of the load. Also, the neck is tougher than the shoulders and can sustain a load for a longer time. On the debit side they cannot swing their heads or get more than a very restricted view.

This traverse led to a formidable rock buttress up which we could hardly believe the route went. It was a place for a rope, we thought, but they waved it aside. The women climbed in their bare feet, probably to save the yakskin soles of their boots on the sharp rock, but whatever the reason it was soon obvious that they were very much at home on the crags, even with sixty-pound loads. But we died a thousand deaths watching them, imagining all too vividly what would happen if one peeled off—the body hurtling downward to be smashed on the debris of the glacier below.

It was astonishing to see how the women used their feet, spreading their prehensile toes and gripping with them as if they were fingers. Every upward movement was studied and carefully controlled. There was no panic as they mounted for 200 feet what would be classed in Britain or the Alps as a difficult rock climb.

The 'crux' was a corner where the rock bulged, then rose vertically from a sketchy foothold. In this recess Nyma stationed himself and guided each Sherpa round by means of a stick pressed against the rock in lieu of foothold. Each man curled his toe round the stick, bent his neck to his chest to prevent the load slipping, and swung round the difficult bulge. There were no scared faces, but for the first and only time in the expedition Kharab Joe's girl friend Huma was without a smile. Most of them seemed to think the climb was a great lark.

Above this the angle eased to another rake zigzagging to a niche between precipices—not a place for sleepwalking. It was four o'clock and we had apparently arrived at a camping place, for there were caves and hollows to shelter some of our team. Water was reasonably close at hand and we were fairly safe from stonefall—though the coolies threw themselves to the ground when one did take place. The stones shone like diamonds as they pinged through the air for a couple of thousand feet to whistle into the depths of the couloir we had recently abandoned for the rock wall.

Our height now we judged to be about 18,000 feet, and the situation was impressive. Immediately behind us, to the north, was a rock face cradling a narrow glacier hanging like a frozen waterfall. On the south side, across the rubble we had marched on all day, were the rock needles we had likened to the Cuillin of Skye. Now they were seen to be formidable mountains in their own right, yet they were mere outliers of the ice ranges behind them. South-west of us, blocking the whole valley, was the Kanchenjunga-like mass that blocked our path and forced us to make this detour. Ideally we should have contoured up the icefall under this face if we were to make the most direct approach to the Tesi Lapcha, but how impracticable this route was we now fully appreciated, for the cataract of ice was riven and contorted between narrow and dangerous walls.

The Rolwaling folk had no eyes for any of this. They were hard at work removing stones and digging out holes to make caves or sleeping quarters for the night. We gave the women our bungalow tent and were glad to turn in to our own without

85

undue lingering, for a wind had risen, forcing us into our sleeping bags to get warm—the first time on the trip that we had foregone supper rather than stay out in the cold.

To our amazement, when we went out to see how the Sherpas were faring we found a number of them lying under the sky with no more cover than their homespuns. They were asleep, and when we asked them in the morning if they had been cold they shook their heads and said they had been warm. They must undoubtedly be among the toughest people in the world. For me that night was the most comfortable I have ever spent in a high camp, and proof that acclimatisation was coming at last.

To awake in this eyrie and look out on a cloudless sky was to get what we had prayed for in the crossing. All going well we should be on the other side of the pass by nightfall. Everyone was in high spirits except two firewood carriers whose luggage had now been used up. By agreement they were now due to return, but they wanted to stay and were downcast when we refused their request.

By half-past eight we had said goodbye to them and begun the climb to an arch of granite curving against the blue sky a long way above us. There were traces of yak dung on these slabs, and we learned with amazement that despite avalanche danger and stonefall yaks are sometimes brought up the couloir and manhauled up the admittedly easy slabs of rock and scree we were now climbing. No one can say that the Sherpas are not enterprising.

From the summit of this rock crest we looked down into a great glacier basin draining a spectacular array of snow peaks, and not for a moment or two did we realise that this glacier was in fact the upper part of the huge rubble-covered ice-field we had been following for the best part of two days. We had bypassed its séracs and crevasses by climbing over this rock wall, and we would have to descend to it again, where it was now a shining highway curving into an infinity of unknown mountains.

Over the glacier we could see the pass over the main range—a narrow saddle between two sharp ice peaks, a cleft defended on one side by a thick wedge of green ice that topped a line of cliffs like icing on a cake, and on the other by an icefall. This was the Tesi Lapcha. It was even more of a mountaineering route than we had supposed. We descended into the wide glacier basin in a traverse of a mile of boulders and slabs, dropping a thousand feet to find ourselves surrounded by glistening peaks. We crossed the glacier, sinking deeply into the surface snow, and climbed up towards the pass.

Dawa Tenzing was excited here, for he had been at this very place with Shipton and Hillary in 1951 and 1952, and he pointed out to us where their party of three sahibs and four Sherpas had turned up this glacier where it swung north-east, to have a look at what lay round the corner. In passing they had climbed the sharp ice peak forming the south flank of the Tesi Lapcha, an example of the skirmishing type of mountaineering in which Shipton excels, demonstrating his abounding energy and instinctive topographical sense of going to the right place. What a wealth of knowledge of this hitherto unknown region of Nepal he has brought back from only two expeditions! And what a brilliant piece of work was his party's reconnaissance of the Everest route which paved the way for the Swiss and for the final climb!

Some of the Sherpas without sun glasses were suffering from the glare here, and it was interesting to see their natural way of overcoming it. They merely took strands of their long hair and pulled it over their eyes, and very effective blinkers this improvisation seemed to make. While they took a meal of tsampa we examined the icefall up which we would have to climb.

We were in luck. The surface that could so easily have been clear ice, involving us in hard step-cutting, was covered with a layer of firm snow giving good foothold. By keeping well to the left side of the pass we would clear all obstacles. After an initial steepness the slope rose evenly to a shoulder. This was a slope that Hillary had found difficult with clear ice, so we congratulated ourselves on our good fortune.

The heavily laden Rolwaling folk found this lift very hard, for with sixty- and seventy-pound loads they were grossly overburdened for climbing at this unaccustomed altitude. But they went up with a will and made height steadily towards the gap between the mountains. On our north side a great sheet of reddish granite shot to a pinnacle. Flanking us on the other side was Shipton's peak, a soaring snow-point trailing a plume of spindrift which stung our faces as we got into its backlash; this made the going harder, for we sank into drifts caused by it. Sinking deeply and heads down to the wind the women came last, battling gamely on.

It was an inspiring moment to step over the windy col and look on a horizon of new mountains standing above cloud seas and steaming vapours that simmered like porridge in a pot. This was Sola Khombu, the fabled home of the Sherpas, a world of ice, sheer walls and spires, where it seemed only a race of great mountaineers could live, for the visual impact was one of relentless savagery.

It was too cold to linger here. The slope below us bent away icily, swept clear and polished by the wind, making it slippery going for Sherpas with only yakskin soles to their boots. Some of them joined hands for greater stability. Others with axes started to cut steps, the women being particularly nervous and grateful for assistance.

Soon the slope became an ice cliff with gaping folds like an open concertina, but there was a cunning corridor down, with a rocky couloir hard against its edge. Descent of this difficult portion was no more than a steep and slippery scramble, well clear of the natural line of avalanches from above.

Once down the little rock pitches of this place we were on a gentle incline, then another icefall bent steeply away. Local knowledge was invaluable here, for Dawa Tenzing knew exactly the outlet to choose from this high basin, and soon we were plunging down broken rocks and scree, crossing ice patches and descending snow slopes to another hanging corrie.

Temper-breaking work began here, for the whole lower part of the corrie was treacherously loose, piled high with rubble as far as we could see. Keeping as far as possible to a rock shoulder, we kept traversing to the right, to hit a moraine like an embankment which was firmer under foot. It took us down to about 16,000 feet, to a tangle of rock-strewn hillocks which we could not avoid, where we were forced up and down over their steep sides—back-breaking work for the coolies at the end of such a hard day's carrying. How they found energy to cross this unstable mass I shall never know. We were tired carrying only fifteen pounds each, yet the Rolwaling people had been carrying more than a normal Sherpa load all day.

It seemed an eternal wilderness of stones but at last we came to a cairn, then to a path leading to grass, and the first welcome slope where we could descend comfortably to a glen with a stream and thankfully select a camp site.

The place was good enough to be a mirage—a hollow with caves and dwarf juniper to provide heat and shelter for our whole band. One by one they struggled in, tired, but not too tired to give us a salaam when we shouted 'shabash' (good show) for a truly great day's work. They had been carrying for ten hours, and as we issued them with a baksheesh in the form of tea, sugar, soup and pemmican we told them they could take a long lie in the morning and get their strength back after such a fine lift.

We were in grand spirits. The Tesi Lapcha had been a high-light of the expedition, a superbly interesting pass, and now we were in the Sola Khombu country with Everest just round the corner. There was gaiety and laughter round the little fires twinkling in the dark, and we could hear the slap of chapattie-making and the busy clatter of cooking. Above us the moon was a pale sickle glistening on a ribbon of snow 5,000 feet sheer above, and we felt with the coolies in their song that life was good.

There was a delightful holiday feeling abroad the following day. The morning was like spring. The grass glistened in the sun with melting frost and high overhead ridges of snow peaks stretched immensely to the Tibetan sky, tiny gentians peeping here and there from the brown turf. Flocks of mountain finches like linnets twittered in the still air.

Since it felt like spring we thought it was time we did ourselves the honour of having a clean up, and at a respectable distance from the camp we stripped and had our first decent wash for a week. We would have been content to dawdle longer in this idyllic spot but our Sherpas, normally eager to co-operate, were hurrying the Rolwaling men and women to get packed up. The explanation was, of course, that they could hardly wait to get to their homes, which were only a short distance away. So though we offered a half-holiday no one wanted it.

We were on the move by ten o'clock, on a path winding down a glen which was rapidly becoming a ravine. Beyond its depths, and high above, were the snow peaks we had seen from the top of the pass, now clear of cloud from base to summit, impossible-looking peaks with razor edges ending in slender ice pinnacles or blunt turrets too sheer-walled to offer hope to mortal moun-taineers. These were the home peaks of our men and they pointed them out with pride, particularly the Mustah Tower shape of Amadablam which pinpointed Namche Bazar for them.

Very early that morning Ang Dawa had left us to go to his home at Thami to have a few hours with his people until our caravan passed through his village. To our surprise we now saw him coming up the path to meet us. His salaam was as ceremonious as if he had not seen us for years. Respectfully he asked us if we would sit down, at which off came his rucksack and out came boiled eggs and a wooden bottle of raxi.

It was a kindly thought. Instead of taking his ease at home he must have gone at the double to get these refreshments for us and started back straight away. We did not think much of Ang Dawa as a porter but we liked him, for he was a fine youngster of high intelligence and much given to reading. We thought him a shirker, but the truth was that he should never have been sent to us as a load-carrier, for he suffered from some physical infirmity that was aggravated as the expedition progressed, and from this day of his touching present to us we watched his normal cheery expression decline to a stricken look of pain. His spirit was willing enough and he did not look weak, but no amount of medicine we gave him seemed to do any good.

Having heard so much of Sola Khombu it was interesting to come to the first villages perched on green alps under the most massive rock and ice walls we had ever seen. They were deserted except for alpine choughs. Tall prayer flags fluttered in the breeze, but the people, like most of the birds, were away to a warmer clime. The Sherpas who live here in summer must shudder at the roar of many an ice avalanche hurtling down so close to them, but what a charming spot in which to spend the finest months of the year, when every meadow is carpeted with flowers, in a temperature that is seldom too hot or too cold.

Moving steadily downward we came amongst waterfalls and the first scrubby trees, ragged with lingering autumn colours. Perched Tibetan fashion on a cliff above us was Thami Gompa, which was the destination of the lama who had accompanied us. He was already inside it and busy at his prayers when we climbed up to look in. The place was deserted, most of the monks being over in Tibet at Rongbuk.

Below the sacred yew trees and pink gompa buildings was the main village, situated on a level patch above the confluence of two rivers. The northerly one of these was the main route to Tibet by the Nangpa La, three marches away. This Sherpa village promised outstanding photographic opportunities, with its grinning Tibetans, masses of sheep, goats and yaks, and white-washed houses square and well built. But the people were not so unsophisticated as they looked, and when we tried to mani-pulate some of them into a photograph they demanded money before they would pose. We walked off in disgust. National expeditions loaded with unlimited funds may mean 'pie in the sky' but we had no intention of rousing false expectations here or anywhere else. Our funds were already very low and would be lower still if these Sherpas got their way. Luckily Ang Dawa's house was not in the village but was a stone hut situated in a corner of a steep hillside where we could camp in privacy while the Sherpas made free in the kitchen.

To be in Sola Khombu again had raised the spirits of our Sherpas markedly. They were like schoolboys and could hardly contain themselves at the thought that tomorrow they would be on holiday in Namche Bazar. The simple little house was packed to capacity when we looked in, and a torrent of talking and laughing greeted us when we opened the door. Over a fire in the middle of the floor pots of thick tsampa and bubbling rice and lentils were just waiting to be served. There are no caste taboos about food with Sherpas, and far from resenting our presence they welcomed it. Soon there was hardly any talking as each man and woman got a brass plate of food and delved in with scooping fingers. They sat cross-legged on mats, for there was not a scrap of furniture in the room; in the firelight it was a happy festive scene, but the smoke and fug were too much for us and we beat a retreat into the dark night to weigh our finances and discuss future mountain plans.

Finances are the bugbear of private expeditions. We had allowed ourselves roughly £350 each for this trip, and although we had been in the hills for only forty days or so, our cash was already low enough to be a cause of some anxiety. Any idea we may have had of climbing a larger peak than any we had met so far was now out of the question.

The perfect coat to fit our cloth now would be a trek into the Everest region, with a small peak thrown in, if such we could find. Whatever happened we wanted to see the monster at close range, and we would have the pleasure of walking up the gorges draining the mountain which Shipton thought the most beautiful he had ever seen. By way of finish to our campaign we might try to make a new route back to Katmandu and add something original to the exploration of the country. With this rough plan formed we went to bed.

The route next day followed a winding path along the north wall of the Bhote Kosi, entering a region where the soft green of cypress and pine mingled with red and yellow shrubs, and on every bank were cushions of gentians. In contrast to our smiling world of colour and sunshine we looked into the depth of a gorge so profound as to be in perpetual shadow. On the heights around us were houses—white dots like Highland clachans—with yaks, sheep and goats foraging on the bare fields round them.

Every few hundred yards we had to detour to pay religious observance to large boulders carved from top to bottom with the usual prayers, a mortification of the flesh to heavily laden men, but a matter of duty that no Buddhist will shirk however heavily laden. In contradiction to the teaching of the Buddha, every Tibetan-robed Sherpa we met stopped us to ask for cigarettes or baksheesh, and a girl refused to allow a photograph until she had first been given a present. Already we were beginning to feel a bit cynical about Sola Khombu.

Suddenly, on rounding a bend, we looked down on the white squares of houses built one above the other on the steep curve of a recess above the mighty gorge of the Dudh Kosi (Milk River). Glittering ice peaks ringed it round—a man's country, and cynicism was gone in that view which embodied for me the whole romance of the Himalaya and the great race of mountaineering Sherpas who wrest a living from below its stupendous peaks.

Some of our men were already down there, and the whole populace was waiting to greet us, with tumblers of chang and raxi (rice spirit), and dainty cups of Tibetan butter-tea which looked better than it tasted. We were being salaamed in all directions by grinning men and women dressed in an amazing collection of clothes, from spiv suits and homespuns to fine climbing breeches and eiderdown 'Everest' jackets. Several were already intoxicated and we assumed it was by over-indulgence in our honour. We did not know then that chang and raxi drinking is the favourite pastime in Namche, and as the liquor of the country is cheap enough to be accessible to all, it has its addicts.

While we talked to the Sherpas and shook hands with an invading host of new arrivals the Sherpas were busy erecting the tents on the dusty soil of a potato field right in the centre of the village. Apart from disliking to have our actions over-looked by everyone in the village we had no intention of risking sore throats from infected dust blown from the village fields, and there was disappointment when we announced our intention of finding a camp spot where there was grass and privacy. The best spot seemed to be a ridge some 600 feet above the village, and though we were assured that there was no water, our intention was to go on until we found some.

With men, women and children carrying bits of our gear we climbed in procession up the steep slope to the ridge and found a good place. There was no need to worry about water. One little woman of middle age appointed herself water-carrier and climbed up the hillside chatting to me and carrying an enormous water stoup that I could barely move off the ground. How she carried it up that 600-foot slope is something that baffles comprehension, but hardly were we in camp than she went away for another.

There is something very tiring about being stared at by a large number of people. After they had helped us up the slope we did not want to be impolite by telling them to clear off, yet we would get no peace while they invaded the tents and found interest in every scrap of equipment lying around. Tom MacKinnon was past caring, for he was unwell, and zip-fastened his tent against all comers. At length we used the same tactics and they took the hint—all but a few young and rather attractive girls who sat around, hoping, but even they became tired in time.

CHAPTER NINE

THE HOME OF THE SHERPA—FLESHPOTS
AND FRUSTRATIONS

OCTOBER 29th was George's birthday, and as this day had to be a holiday to celebrate the Sherpa's homecoming to their native land we celebrated it in style ourselves. A birthday in Scotland is an occasion for a dumpling, so this very special day we mixed up suet, butter, sugar, honey, raisins, etc., in preparation for a feast. In 1950 we had made our dumplings in my old pyjamas, but on this trip, with the aid of the pressure cooker, we were turning out much more professional efforts.

Between times we paid off the Rolwaling folk, and we had real regrets at parting. So had they, and would have preferred to stay with us, but it is better when travelling to engage men with knowledge of the district rather than have a party of strangers, so our preference was for Namche men. Unladen, the Rolwaling men and women would probably shoot across the Tesi Lapcha in half the time it had taken us, and we wished them luck.

Most of the day we were besieged by Namche men, some looking for jobs, some on the hunt for baksheesh, others merely curious, especially the women, who were prepared to sit out as long as daylight lasted. Yet if we spoke to them they merely looked embarrassed and giggled. Some of the men who had come down from the hills to look for work with us were truly delightful, and we engaged them in preference to the more sophisticated types, who in our experience are too often trouble-makers.

Dawa Tenzing's wife, who had the reputation of being a witch, had arrived with them, and was soon sharing his tent and wearing his red tartan shirt. She was a strong-looking woman, well past her first youth but still exuding charm. Her ears were almost hidden by tinsel frying-pan ornaments and her wrists and neck were covered with beads. Wives, lovers, friends were so hopelessly intermingled that it was hard to identify who was who, but when it came to asking names we discovered that the Tenzings are the Smiths of Sola Khombu, and also that if you see a married Sherpa holding hands with a girl there is no need to assume that she is his wife.

Douglas Scott had been on a photographic prowl and came back exhausted, but impressed by what he had seen of Namche's double-storied houses and the fine rugs and clothing kept within. When he went to take a photograph of a man and wife they had insisted on dressing up for him and sitting outside their house on carpets, complete with small dog, small baby and Tibetan teacups. The man wore red silk trousers embroidered with fine designs, with a fur hat to match. The woman wore a gorgeous apron over a cloak like a dressing gown but with sleeves of silk. George had been visiting the local bootmaker to order Tibetan boots for himself.

The dumpling was the next item on the agenda, and was accompanied by a reading from the works of Robert Burns by George, who on the occasion of his birthday applied 'Chieftain o' the puddin' race' to this particular Himalayan creation. That night, as was appropriate to the occasion, we went to a party, and were escorted there through the darkness of Namche by Dawa and Nyma.

The party was in our young Sherpa Kamin's house. We elbowed our way through sleeping yaks on the pitch-black bottom floor to climb up a steep ladder into the cosy glow of a blazing fire and the bright flame of a torch of resinous wood.

97

We were the first arrivals and were invited to sit on a bench near the fire while a service of Tibetan tea and chang was brought round.

Considering there was no chimney to the fireplace the room was remarkably smoke-free. It escaped by a hole in the far corner of the roof and the resin-charged torch used for light gave no smoke at all. The torch had to be replenished every few minutes with fresh splinters from a log kept specially for the purpose. We were thinking that Tom should have brought some bandages with him, for the youngster who cut these splinters used a kukri, making downward-slanting blows at the log, which was held in position between her toes. One false move and she would have been collecting her toes off the floor.

It was a large room broken into three main divisions by carved wood frames and with newspapers as wallpaper. Beyond the kitchen was the drawing-room-cum-shebeen, with rugs on the floor, little ornaments and decorations, and casks of chang and raxi. Opposite the fireplace the windowless far wall seemed occupied entirely by household pots, pans, stoups for water or grain, and great copper basins. Beyond the drawing-room was the third division, in the form of a warehouse, with sacks of grain, bales of wool, rolls of carpet, and other stuffs of the summer trade with Tibet. We were obviously in a wealthy house, part pub, part warehouse, and part dwelling house.

Sherpas and Sherpanis arrived in twos and threes during the next half hour, and we heard the clink of rupees as each paid the dues for the delights that were to follow. The party like many another began solemnly, but self-consciousness was dispelled as the chang cups circulated. We gave a tune on the mouth organ and Nyma started to sing, but his doleful air nearly sent us to sleep.

We urged them to dance, but it seemed they had not yet had enough to drink, and there was a cheer when at last some men took the floor, each with an arm round the other's waist, swaying to the rhythm of a doleful song struck up by the leading singer, an air not unlike a Gaelic dirge and with as many verses. We were thinking they took their pleasures sadly when suddenly there was a change of tempo, and instead of the slow blues they now stamped their feet like jitterbugs to a four-beat rhythm that was pure jazz. Wound up to a high pitch of excitement they now changed from song to a syncopated arrangement of hissing sounds in an improvisation that a jazz fan would have called a 'hot chorus.' The arrangement was ingenious, and had an obvious pattern, for the footwork was complicated yet executed with the utmost precision by one and all of the dancers; it was not unlike the Charleston.

All the time this went on there was a running buffet of chang and rice spirit, each dancer draining his cup at a gulp and continuing the figure with hardly an interruption in his movements. It was interesting to watch the mounting excitement of the dancers, whose movements became less and less inhibited as the chang took its effect.

But for the spectators the songs and movements kept too much to a pattern. Having heard one we had heard the lot, and after an hour or two of it we took ourselves off to bed. It is possible that by so doing we missed the best of it, for by the time we left the dancers were downing their liquor in double-charges, and at four o'clock we could still hear the sounds of merriment floating up to our tents.

The effects were apparent in the morning. No one wanted to work. Indeed the only lively thing in camp was a sheep we had purchased to be killed and consumed when we reached the Everest region, but no one would consent to lead it. We were fast reaching a state of exasperation for it was now ten o'clock and the new coolies we had engaged were still picking up and dropping loads, hoping to find a nice light one. A show of force was indicated. We each grabbed a coolie, led him to a load and stood over him until he lifted it. The sheep could be left, so far as we cared, and we said so, but when we looked back the man who had sold us it was leading it himself, anxious apparently not to be done out of a sale.

Wrangling with coolies is the most objectionable aspect of Himalayan travel and this had been a particularly gruelling morning, but our annoyance was dispelled at once. Once clear of the ridge we looked on an enormous curtain of rock ribboned by a crest of snow rising to a blunt pyramid. 'Chomolungma,' said a Sherpa voice at my side. We were looking at the 'Mother of the Snows,' the great Everest itself. The Sherpas believe this to be the most beautiful region in the Himalayas. We could only agree. There was a perfection in that view we had not expected.

Everything was so perfectly proportioned. Far below us was the gorge of the Dudh Kosi twisting in a deep ravine of pines which framed the tremendous tower of Amadablam, so clear and sparklingly vivid that we were seeing every detail of its impregnable cornices and knife-edge ridges. On the other side of the ravine was the face of Lhotse, perhaps the greatest mountain wall in the world, plunging from 28,000 feet to the Imja Khola in one 12,000-foot sweep. The south-east ridge of Everest looked a walk-over from this aspect, but just how deceptive that impression was we know now that the mountain has been climbed.

The route ahead was drawn like an immense curve on the north wall of the gorge, dipping down out of sight at one point and rising again to an alp on which rose like a rock peak the gilded summit of a Buddhist monastery called Thyangboche. It looked near in that crystal atmosphere, where a hundred miles can look like ten at home, but we felt we had done a fair march by the time we had dropped 2,000 feet and risen another

3,000 through pine trees to the alp. People familiar with misty British hills where distances turn out to be shorter than they seem often remark on how deceptive are Alpine distances, where the opposite rule prevails. They would find the same disparity between Alpine and Himalayan distances, and it is one of the factors that make reconnaissance of Himalayan peaks so difficult where the problem of scale is constantly perplexing.

We did not see Thyangboche at its best that afternoon, owing to a drizzling mist that crept down as we climbed to it. But it did not spoil our enjoyment of this splendid camp site, and we honoured George's birthday a second time with a huge omelette followed by tinned salmon, potatoes and rice, fresh guavas and caramel pudding. One by one the Sherpas straggled in, and lost no time in heading up to the gompa. As prayer is a long and serious business there is never any lack of refreshment in the way of chang and raxi, and our Sherpas were quick to seize every opportunity of spiritual communion.

The full beauty of our position burst on us when we looked out over green sward to the tapering pile of gleaming white and pink buildings which is Thyangboche Gompa. This morning its gilt summit was encircled by rock and ice peaks, and yaks grazed peacefully on the green. Walled to the north-east by Everest and ringed round by the gorges of the Dudh Kosi, the Bhote Kosi and the Imja Khola, we felt that here was the ideal spot for a life of contemplation of heaven and earth. Just as the Rongbuk Monastery served spiritually and practically every expedition that went to the north side of Everest, so was this monastery of Thyangboche to prove of great value to the Sherpas and sahibs of the successful British Expedition.

We paid the gompa a formal visit that morning, having first removed our boots to do honour to a very holy lama who lay buried at the door. For him we lit candles costing a rupee each while the Sherpas prayed and touched the floor with their

101

heads. There were some fine wall paintings and t'hankas (holy scrolls and drawings on cloth), golden images of Buddha, precious stones, devil-dance masks, holy books, drums, horns, and all the other quaint odds and ends of lamastic Buddhism. We went from room to room of this high and commodious building but it felt chill and gloomy in contrast to the warmth and brightness of the outside world. As a last ceremony we went right round the building turning the hundreds of prayer wheels set into its walls.

The alp was a place to linger but we would be returning that way, and we felt we should move while the weather was still good. So in mid-morning we left Thyangboche and swung downhill to the Imja Khola where it bent north-east towards Everest, through woodland dells with leaves of red and orange on gleaming silver birches and through groves of green pines and rhododendrons. Black and yellow grosbeaks flitted across our path here, and the first blood pheasants we had ever seen strutted in the woods, brilliantly coloured in green and red and with the deliberate movements of domestic hens. Douglas would dearly have loved a brace of these birds for the pot, but they were tame because they were protected by the lamas and it would have been sacrilege to throw a stone—we could hardly have missed.

Alongside the path were finely carved mani walls and turning prayer wheels powered by water from little mountain streams. We were on a fine track dropping all the time to the river, which was spanned by a log bridge poised above a considerable force of water. There was no respite in the climbing thereafter, and our porters would have been less than human if they had not been galled by the large number of prayer walls, carved stones and chortens round which they were obliged to climb in order to pass them on their left flank. There were a few hill settlements up here, and the people were busy harvesting the last of the potato crop, or already moving down to evacuate this region for the winter. Caravans of yaks and their wild-looking drovers passed us continually, laden with what looked like household provisions.

From the Imja Khola we turned north, changing direction where another glen cut down the wild glacial region draining Mount Everest. We were within a day's march of the Swiss Base Camp, and there was evidence of where they had camped when we came on a dump of cardboard cartons filled with rubbish. Every day since we had been in the mountains we had been wondering how this valiant winter attempt on the mountain was progressing, but even in Namche Bazar no one seemed to know. But we gathered that they were high up and having an uncomfortable time.

It is strange how weakness suddenly descends on a man in the Himalaya. I had started that day feeling well, yet as we climbed up the Chola Khola I found myself like Tom MacKinnon at Namche, looking forward eagerly to lying down. The climb became hateful and never-ending and I began almost to envy the fate of the sheep following in our wake. We camped among the little walled fields of some summer shielings called Palong Kharpo below a finger of rock and ice called Taweeche.

The march had not been a long one, yet we were truly in the heart of the mountains, with a choice of magnificent peaks on every side, for Palong Kharpo is the Chamonix of Nepal, and around us was every conceivable kind of climbing problem, from fantastic rock needles to ice walls and spires of such jagged form that we could not imagine them climbable by any route. Yet I would hazard a guess that these mountains will be climbed in the future, by the next generation of climbers if not by this one. The peak we selected for ourselves was the most modest we could see, mostly grass with a rocky top, its height no more than 18,000 feet at most.

We set off for it next day, and it was a grand little expedition, giving us a view into that country which had so enthralled Shipton when he saw this new aspect of peaks and saddles so familiar to him from Rongbuk; Pumori, Lingtren, the Lho La, North Peak and west shoulder of Everest. We looked down on the grey desert of the Khombu glacier, pinnacled with ice and bending round into the hidden Western Cwm, the scene that Mallory described as 'one of the most awful and utterly forbidding scenes ever observed by man,' when he first saw it from the Lho La in 1924. We agreed, yet our hearts were up there with him as we looked on the ultimate point where earth and sky met more than 12,000 feet above our heads. We could not look unmoved at this focal point of such high endeavour and we knew what Mallory would have given to be in our shoes, to read the answer to a topographical riddle that he more than anyone nearly solved; it was ultimately to be solved by the efforts of Swiss, New Zealand and British climbers.

Acclimatisation is a rare reward in the Himalaya, worth striving for however long it may take, and we proved we were fit by climbing the peak and being back in camp by 3.30 p.m., though the knowledge that we were due for a leg of our sheep may have been responsible for this turn of speed. This would be the first fresh meat put before us since leaving Katmandu and we were going to make up for our abstinence, though we felt sorry for the poor beast that had walked all of twenty miles and climbed some 5,000 feet to give us this banquet—and banquet it was, for the mutton was delicious.

But its killing was no casual affair, and in the darkness we found the Sherpas had erected a small altar and were gathered round it chanting prayers before a butter lamp illuminating it. This was a serious matter evidently. Each man held his left palm before him, little finger and forefinger erect, the other fingers clenched on some rice held in the hollow of the palm to be thrown towards the candle at each new series of prayers The prayers went on until the candle was burnt out.

The ceremony was of course for the sheep they had killed, for the taking of life is against the Buddhist religion and animals can only be slaughtered with the safeguard of prayer. Normally there are days appointed by the lamas for killing, when with the proper safeguards of prayer the souls of the animals killed are promoted to a higher life. This ceremony was intended presumably to justify the life taken outside the normal calendar, and to placate the soul within the sheep, whose reincarnation to a better life would be assured. The conscience of Sherpas is very delicate in such matters, and it genuinely upsets them to kill even a hen, or watch anything being killed.

That night was one of the coldest we had in any camp, yet we could not remain in our sleeping bags for looking out again and again at the moon shining on the pale tops of peaks that projected high above the clouds—ghostly shapes of another world rather than the roof of our own planet. It made us think of the Swiss, lying somewhere up there at this moment on the ice of the Lhotse face. Strung out over the 10,000 feet of Everest that was their battle ground, they were enduring some of the most trying conditions men have ever faced in order to climb a mountain. How they stuck out these long winter nights we could not imagine, yet despite setbacks of deep snow and accident they were pressing their attack, for our Sherpas told us that they had just despatched porters to Katmandu 150 miles away to bring back fresh supplies of food and kerosene. The world should not readily forget this tour de force of the Swiss which contributed so much to the final climb.

Long frost feathers hung from the roof of the tents and the canvas was stiff as wood when I parted the door curtains at four o'clock for another look outside. Every trace of cloud had gone and every peak stood clear cut in silhouette. The moon seemed poised on the very point of an incredibly sharp rock spire, which even as I looked pierced it through, skewering it like an apple on a stick. As this would be our last true mountain camp I lay awake waiting for the dawn, and it was well worth waiting for—not sensationally red but softly gold, touching the snow peaks one by one, flooding over their crests in a spill of racing warmth that lit rock faces and moraine stones in a wave of intense energy spent almost in the instant of its touching.

We would have liked to spend a week in this delightful spot instead of taking the road south, back to Thyangboche, but the press of poverty is an over-ruling force. I got a fright at one point on this march, when I descended through a thicket of rhododendron and startled a party of yaks which were invisible to me until there was a crash of vegetation and wild-eyed hairy brutes with handlebar horns exploded in all directions, snorting not with anger but with fear. Another interesting encounter was with a polecat carrying what looked like a live tail-less rat in its mouth. More Sherpas seemed to have arrived in the high villages here, for every field had its potato harvesters, and a great digging was in progress. The date was early November, and after the barley and potato harvest these highest villages in the world would be evacuated until spring.

But even if we were sorry to leave the heights it was a pleasure to enter the tree zone of Thyangboche again, and climb up through these colourful woods to emerge once more on the alp below the gompa for a last magic camp. As though to celebrate our arrival a fierce clashing of cymbals and blowing of horns sounded, and to a man (and woman) our porters answered the call to the chang pots. It was very late and they were very merry when they returned.

There was an autumnal feeling in the air next morning, a subtlety of colour in the woods and a soft unsharpness that gave mysterious aloofness to the peaks coming and going out of masses of drifting clouds. For the first time we had the true feeling of scale, of the depth and height of this country, as we looked down through layer after layer of cloud to the canyon bluffs of the Dudh Kosi, its stream glimpsed as a waterfall plunging into dark and unknown depths, or up to Everest, its pyramid just clear of cloud which streamed like a snow-plume from its south-eastern ridge. It took this gauzy unsharpness and veiling cloud to reveal what a plunge from 29,000 feet to 10,000 means, in impression more powerful to the imagination than any photograph. Scarlet leaves with the brightness of blossom overflowed the edge of our green alp, giving us the feeling that we were indeed on a magic carpet in space.

To be a photographer on such a morning was a penance; one felt such a sense of hopelessness in trying to capture the magic of the scene, made up of so many fragments, and so magically distilled with a non-photographic substance called atmosphere. Nevertheless we tried, and the results in colour were better than we had hoped for. High in the air we saw little flights of birds new to us this trip—Himalayan nutcrackers, like small magpies in their chattering flight and contrasting black and white.

We were going to Kumjung now, not to Namche, for most of our porters came from there, and according to them it was the Sherpa paradise of the Himalaya. We felt we could lose nothing by going there since it would need to be bad to be worse than Namche, for romantic as that place was, we felt we had seen enough of its inquisitive and too sophisticated people to want to go back in a hurry.

The first part of the march was familiar, down a steep jungle face for 3,000 feet to the Dudh Kosi, then up 2,000 feet on the far bank, to climb through glades where rose-finches, noisy babblers and flocks of white-cheeked and variegated thrushes flew busily. The finest sight was a grey cliff that suddenly blossomed with the white wings of hundreds of snow pigeons which whirled over us to land again with a rippling flutter on the cliff from which they had taken off.

The fiery cross warning the Kumjung clan of our arrival must have preceded us, for we were met at the junction of the path by Dawa's wife and children, and an assortment of village men and maidens who took our baggage and climbed with us into a corrie with a triple rock peak as crest. The village occupied a delightful perch, looking out to Thyangboche, which gleamed so near that we could hardly credit that it was fully half a day's march away. In the now sparkling clear air it appeared to be perched not on its own alp but on the slope of Amadablam, in a Himalayan over-simplification of landscape. In another direction we could see that what looked like one peak was in fact three telescoped by the clarity of the air.

Politeness decreed that our first duty in Kumjung was to accept the hospitality of the Sherpas who had homes there, and to begin with we were led to Dawa Tenzing's place, a house in shape and construction like the others in Kumjung, with the same spaciousness upstairs as the one described in Namche. But Dawa's was more of a workshop and less of a shebeen than the Namche one. Indeed the place was a hive of activity.

By the light of finely carved lattice windows a couple of girls were combing wool with needle-sharp brushes, while an ancient dame worked at a carpet on a large wood-framed loom. Others were busy at cooking pots, while Mrs Dawa filled a large wooden bottle with raxi from a barrel in preparation for a round of toasts. Ornaments from many expeditions in which Dawa had taken part were presented to us for inspection and it was soon obvious that this was a very well set-up establishment indeed.

Before we came out of the house it was snowing and the mist had clamped down—evidently the unusual splendour of that morning had been the sign of impending change. It became a foul night and we did not venture out again.

It was a dull white and strangely shrunken world we looked out on next morning, with Amadablam looking scarcely higher than the Matterhorn from Zermatt, until a warm sun came out and thawed out the surrounding alps sufficiently to restore colour to the glens and add sparkling height again to the peaks. Apparently the only heavy snowfalls of the year in Kumjung take place in January and February, but are not inconvenient enough to drive the population down to lower levels.

There was much to do in preparation for our move on the following day. Baggage would have to be weighed, porters interviewed and given an advance of pay, and food supplies checked to ensure that we had enough to take us back to Katmandu, for it was our intention to return by a northern route unfamiliar to our Sherpas, which meant that we could not depend on obtaining local supplies.

When Nyma arrived with his coolies it was immediately clear that we had more than enough for two expeditions of our kind. To our astonishment he had sacked the Kumjung men who had been such good companions for the past week, and it did not take a particularly discerning eye to see that what he was now saddling us with was a mixed bag of friends, relations and girl friends. Even Dawa's wife and daughter were proposing to come with us as coolies, and Mingma had arrived with his wife, who was prepared to carry a little baby in addition to a sixty-pound load.

We had no intention of seeing our old friends left in the lurch, but we asked Nyma to line up his team of coolies so that we could sort out the potential carriers from the hangers-on. In numbers they were four to five more than our requirements and we asked him what he meant by giving us fifteen when we had asked for ten. He shrugged his shoulders and pretended that he did not understand my Hindustani, which was an infuriating trick he practised when it suited him.

We looked then at the eager faces of the Sherpas who until yesterday had been working for us and had now been discarded. Three of them were simple types and the fourth was little Passang, who had been with us since Katmandu, a dwarfish fellow with a chest like a barrel and a tremendous capacity for hard work.

'Why are you not taking these men?' we asked Nyma, pointing to our old friends. His reply that they were 'no use' staggered us, for Passang had carried the heaviest load of any man over the Tesi Lapcha.

There was only one thing to be done, and that was over-rule him. We pushed out these four and singled out Kharab Joe and Huma, who had likewise been sacked, but such an acrimonious argument developed here that we allowed Nyma to have his way, leaving Joe and Huma downcast. Mingma's wife, complete with baby, we allowed to stay, for we liked Mingma, and for the same reason we took Dawa's sixteen-year-old daughter but rejected his wife, to Dawa's secret delight.

It was pleasant to have time to ourselves in the afternoon, and we spent it on photography and on being entertained at Passang's house with a meal of potatoes and rice washed down with buttermilk; in return we gave some tunes on the mouth organ. This was a well-ordered house, so neat and tidy that a British housewife might have been proud of it. The manners of Passang and his sisters were in keeping with it, in contrast to those at Dawa's, which we revisited later.

There was no buttermilk here. The 'hard stuff' was flowing, and 'torch' songs were being sung solo by Dawa's semi-inebriated wife. As each guest arrived he was ceremoniously seated and the lady of the house approached with a glass of raxi. Standing front of him she sang a high-pitched welcome in a piercing wail, ending with herself drinking some of the spirits while the guest took the remainder at a gulp. For the hostess it seemed a pretty good way to begin a party. At two o'clock, long after we were in bed, we could still hear the wailing songs floating down from Dawa's house and knew we were going to have trouble getting away in the morning.

We were quite correct. It took us from six till half-past eight to get the porters moving, and would have taken longer but for the intervention of Dawa Tenzing, who saw we were being driven to desperation by this waste of a superb morning.

But again we had that delicious feeling of release when once we got going, for this was a walk of a lifetime, and the memory of the descent from these alps of Kumjung to the gorge of the Dudh Kosi is something we shall always treasure. We followed a winding path through groves of birch and rhododendron, with chir pines dotting the ridge crests and acting as a frame for a horizon filled by Everest and Amadablam.

We blessed the Sherpas who had led us to this corrie slung between two magnificent gorges—a hanging corrie of brown alps with gentians under our feet. The lip of the corrie curled down to the junction of the gorges, which marked the parting of our ways. We had come to Everest from the east; now we must bend south with the Dudh Kosi, down its defile to where the sky had the milky shimmer of the Indian Plains and not the pale and frosty blue of the roof of Tibet.

It was a sad thought to be leaving this, and we talked of how it must be to live in Kumjung for a year, seeing the pattern of the seasons, watching the alps turn from the brown of winter to the verdant green of spring, with flowers we remembered from Garhwal blooming everywhere, yellow potentillas, blue geraniums, alpine saxifrages, primulas, blue poppies, masses of red rhododendron blossom framing the snows.

How grand it would be to spend the summer exploring the unknown country only three or four marches away! Perhaps we might accompany a Sherpa caravan into Tibet over the

Nangpa La, highest trade route in the world; follow the cycle of
the Sherpas' lives through the seasons; tap their vast store of
local knowledge and folklore; see their ceremonies at birth,
marriage and death. What endeared us to Kumjung and
Rolwaling was the fact that the people had not been westernised.
They were independent of Darjeeling. We would have liked
to have seen their migrations to sow and plant the high fields,
and to visit the summer pastures on the edge of the glaciers with
the yaks, sheep and goats so vital to them for milk and butter,
and wool for clothing. Nor would spending a year in Kumjung
be impossible for a European who could learn to live as
Sherpas do.

Namche seemed an anticlimax after Kumjung, but we were
hospitably entertained by the merchant who was supplying us
with food, and while we plied chopsticks and tried to wriggle
unwieldy strips of tsampa macaroni into our mouths, the weights
of our bags of rice, lentils and tsampa were checked before we
handed over our dues of 180 rupees.

We were now ready for the road, on the last phase of the
expedition.

CHAPTER TEN

CROSS-COUNTRY TO KATMANDU

WIVES, brothers, sisters, children seemed bent on joining our caravan in Namche. Which were coolies and which were merely camp followers it was impossible to tell, for everybody seemed to be carrying something, but all had a common instinct to sit down until prodded to activity.

Tom MacKinnon, who is normally a self-effacing man not given to chivvying anyone, surprised us all by acting the boss. The shock to the coolies was such that they took one look at his fiery beard waggling in their direction and made off. Padding along in the convoy, much to our surprise, was Kharab Joe, carrying not our luggage but his own, plus a present of potatoes for us. Although Nyma refused to have him as a coolie he was coming just the same, for on joining our party at Katmandu he had left some of his surplus gear there, and although it meant a walk of over a hundred miles each way, he was going there to collect it.

Padding along in front of the convoy was Mingma's wife, with her four-months-old baby mounted on top of her huge sixty-pound load. She travelled ahead so that she could stop and suckle the youngster without being left behind the main stream of traffic. We marvelled at her sureness of foot, for the path dropped in fierce zigzags, looping down 1,500 feet in one sweep to the river, then going across it by a log bridge, to climb up what was virtually a staircase hacked out of the crags and buttressed in places by logs of wood cunningly notched to give a grip for the feet.

113

Two or three thousand feet above us, where ravines cut down from the mountains hemming us in, we could see the white dots of Sherpa villages cradled in hanging corries—the homes of some of our men, who pointed them out with glee and invited us to take a walk up to see them. No wonder the Sherpa is such a tireless climber. It made us feel weary even to think of living up there.

There were little settlements down by the river too. Evidence of the warmer climate here was given by a growth of winter wheat in the fields, the first growing crops we had seen in the hills. We had been impressed by the order and neatness of the Sherpas of Namche and Kumjung, both in their persons and in their houses. Down here the Sherpas were more backward and much dirtier in their habits, and the houses were stinking with excreta. But everybody knew everybody, and loads were abandoned for a chang-drinking session in a dingy shebeen buzzing with flies.

The scale of the Dudh Kosi can only be appreciated when you march down it. Looking from Namche towards the foothills it had appeared as a fairly innocent glen, narrow and rocky, it is true, with many interrupting side glens, but the impression was not of extreme fierceness. In the depths of the glen it was another story. Each of these side ravines represents a climb or a considerable detour, so that sometimes when at the end of a day's march you look back on the camp you have started from it appears only a stone's throw away. These side ravines opened into corries with climbable rock and ice peaks of 18,000 and 19,000 feet standing at their heads. A small expedition could have a delightful time exploring the Dudh Kosi ravine by ravine. It would be cheap too, for native food is plentiful in these high Sherpa villages, and there would be no shortage of first-class porters.

A surprise in the upper reaches of the Dudh Kosi was to meet our first Communist. We took him for a beggar, for he had a little one-stringed fiddle and he asked us for baksheesh. Not getting any he became abusive and harangued the Sherpas against us. We did not know a word he was saying but we watched the Sherpas with interest to see how they took his abuse of us. He got a disappointing reception. The more he talked the angrier grew our men, until at last Ela Tenzing became so infuriated that he ran the man out of camp by the scruff of the neck. With signs and gestures the Sherpas told us that this man was a good-for-nothing from Tibet and had been urging them to rise against us. He was certainly backing a loser trying to incite unrest here, for the Sherpas know they have everything to lose and nothing to gain by Communism. Indeed the cost of living is so low in the tax-free valleys of high Nepal that many Tibetans come over from Tibet to spend the winter there, crossing back to their own country only when the trading season begins.

That day we made an important discovery. It was that Mingma was an excellent cook. In self-defence against Nyma I had done most of the cooking since leaving Katmandu, for he was useless except at very elementary dishes. Nyma was now away on leave for a few days and Mingma took over voluntarily. We had delicious mutton cutlets, green peas and potatoes, followed by guavas and custard, then tea and biscuits—a most excellent meal. Henceforth we appointed him cook, and the standard of feeding improved from day to day, especially as we were in a region where chickens were plentiful and so cheap that we had no quibbles about the price. Indeed since Nyma's departure prices had magically dropped 50 per cent.

The greatest delight of these marches was the vast woods rich with autumn colourings and rustling continually with falling leaves, sometimes punctuated by the crashings of langur monkeys swinging about among the branches. Sometimes we climbed 3,000 feet up or dropped 2,000 feet through these woods, entering little alpine dells cushioned with gentians or flashing with waterfalls.   For two days we had seen the village of Jubing where we should cross the Dudh Kosi, but we seemed by our numerous forced detours to be getting no nearer it, though it always seemed just round the next bend.

It seemed indeed to be the most elusive place we had ever tried to reach, final access to it being by a hidden corrie of alps and trees.   Down this corrie we rattled to Jubing—a neat little village of pink-washed houses surrounded by brilliant rice-fields—not a Sherpa settlement but occupied by the typical Nepalis of the lower valleys.   There was no bridge.   It had come down in the monsoon and we were advised to detour to the south, where after plodding through a mile or two of water-logged ricefields we did find a fragile bridge thrown across boulders projecting from the charging grey flood which thunder-ed down from the snows.   Any man falling in there would not live long, and the Sherpas following Tom across the shaky bridge prayed, touching their foreheads and breasts as they incanted.   Suspended high above the bridge from bank to bank were two ropes of orange flowers like huge daisy-chains—signs of harvest festival.

The uphill plod from here to a camp site was a stern 2,500 feet of unremitting toil for the Sherpas, but it got us up out of the heat of the valley to an island of green well provided with firewood.   We had an airy command of the dark ravine we had traversed, with Khombu signposted by the projecting tips of two enormous peaks glowing with pink.

Next day we had the finest march through the foothills with the delight of crossing a pass into country unknown to any of us, Sherpa or sahib—what magnificent country!   A long climb up through woods alive with birds took us to the crest of the pass, to look down on a vast open corrie sloping down in smooth green shelves and dotted with copses that gave it the appearance of well-kept park-land. In the centre of it, like a manor house, were the white squares of a Sherpa settlement. It is without doubt the most charming Himalayan valley I have seen, and the fact that we were among the first Europeans to see it gave it an additional spice.

From a group of chortens mounted on top of the pass we traced out a winding path crossing the Lumding Khola, mounting the opposite hillside and continuing as a slender thread high above the valley floor. The path served the Sherpa villagers of Ringmo and Aalung, and when we descended to a group of houses of Ringmo, reed pipes, horns and drums were sounding from a gompa, so we judged that a marriage must be in progress, for there was a festive air about the place, with men and women wearing their best homespuns.

But we did not camp in the village. A march that starts with a climb is bad psychologically, so we crossed the river and climbed up the opposite slope so that we would have a good start in the morning. It was a good move, leading us at dusk to a little clearing with room for only two tents. We were on our own that night, for the Sherpas had to go elsewhere to find a site for themselves; gathered round a good-going blaze it was cosy to sup our soup and see the patterns of the fir-tops dance in the firelight.

The charm of the first part of the march next day was the unfamiliar joy of walking on the flat, along a path of springy turf so smooth that one could have cantered a pony over it. We might have been walking on a contour line drawn in a curve above the valley that had so enchanted us yesterday. Now when we looked back we saw it as foreground to the snows. Incredibly clear, the peaks of Khombu seemed to spring straight from this valley in a sweep that dismissed the intervening gorge of the Dudh Kosi and drew Everest, Chamlang and Makalu surprisingly close to us; gullies, ridges and snow cornices seemed quite undiminished by distance. Had we not walked through this country we would have had no idea how far away the peaks were.

We traversed a shoulder and looked down on the Beni Khola, into a new valley hardly less beautiful than the one we had left, a comfortable jogging path which led us to a well-set-up village tastefully laid out with carved chortens, prayer walls, prayer flags and a fine gompa which we judged to be of some importance. This was Junbesi village, and as one man the Sherpas laid down their baggage and adjourned for prayers and a service of chang.

It was above Junbesi that we saw the most exciting bird of the expedition—a long-winged hawk that went shooting past us in a low glide and balanced for a moment, rocking on flickering wings. Then away it went, in a flash of black and white, following contours of the ground, in and out of gullies, pausing magically here and there, its wings held out in a flattened V, long legs outstretched. In a great circle it flew round us, scrutinising the hillside at a height of only ten feet above the ground. At close range we saw it was not black and white but had an ashy head and ashy mantle with ebony black primary feathers. Its tail and underparts were white. The legs appeared pinkish red, but that may have been a trick of the warm light. It was a harrier, of course, most probably a pallid harrier, though the impression of red on the legs does not tally with the pallid harrier's yellow ones.

West of Junbesi we entered another glen and camped among pine trees and high rock bluffs near a village called Tumbu. Douglas was in a seventh heaven of rapture with this place, and round the fire that night he proposed a four o'clock start to climb one of the peaks near the head of the pass for a view of the sunrise. Neither Tom nor I felt particularly starved of mountain views, but George was willing to make the effort, and it was arranged that he and Douglas would breakfast in the small hours and be up on the tops for the sunrise.

They were not up quite so early. Certainly they had an early breakfast, but they wisely delayed their departure in order to eat ours as well. They left at six, and Tom and I were away by half-past seven. It was an invigorating morning and the clouds that had upset Douglas' and George's calculations were clearing fast. I even felt like climbing a peak myself, and did so, but unfortunately chose the wrong one for a view, for I was blocked by another minor peak.

By choosing a peak only a couple of miles from my own, Douglas and George claimed the most tremendous view of the expedition. They looked across a vaporous ocean of cloud to a welter of ice peaks stretching from Annapurna to Kanchenjunga and even Kabru. They reckon they saw over 300 miles of mountains, and were still drunk and incoherent with the sight when they joined us.

Unfortunately it was cloudy when we descended into the Likhu Khola, and we were thus prevented from seeing the Rolwaling peaks on which we had been climbing. In particular we had hoped to see Tom's peak, for it was into this ravine he would have come had he made a pass over his mountain to the south. We dropped down to a low part of the Khola, losing a good 6,500 feet in a descent through alps, forest and terraced fields. Chang was on tap at the first house we struck, so everyone was happy. We camped in the flat of a ricefield, and despite our low altitude were not unduly warm.

Dawa Tenzing had a grand idea that night. It was that instead of making breakfast in the morning we should take up the tents and climb the big west wall of the Khola before the sun struck it. We could breakfast in a chang-house several thousand feet above. He did not put it that way exactly, but that was implied.

119

It was the answer to our problem of getting away in the mornings. In future we merely collapsed the tents on top of the Sherpas, and it was noticeable in our mixed company that the men who slept with girls were the worst risers. Now that Nyma was away from his wife, he was keeping close company with a surly-looking Sherpani with the romantic name of Circedoma. They even held hands going along the paths, and Nyma's old sleeping partners had been ousted from the tent by her.

We were now on to a much-used route, and we climbed on a broad path to the last Sherpa settlement we were to see this trip, situated on a broad corrie and called Chyangma. The changhouse referred to by Dawa proved to be a gompa, gaily strung with prayer flags; pink-washed chortens were painted with the all-seeing eyes of Buddha. We made our perch on the green outside the gompa, and in the first warmth of that sparkling morning it was delightful to sit and sunbathe, looking over to the 13,000-foot peaks we had climbed the day before. Some 2,000 feet above us lay the ridge we would need to cross in order to reach the Khimti Khola.

This day had the quality of a spring day in England—a light breeze, cumulus cloud and the grass vivid green, not brown and frosted as on the heights. Even the bird-calls had the excitement of spring, and birds were everywhere—grey drongos, redstarts, tits, laughing thrushes, babblers. Tom and I saw no panorama to compare with the one described by Douglas and George until we reached the crest of the pass and looked northward.

Nothing blocked our view, and every peak of the frontier ridge stood clear, from the north-westerly giant of Manaslu, with the yellowish sheen of distance on its snows, to the glistening wedges of Rolwaling Wall and the near-Matterhorn of Gauri Sankar. But no peak surpassed for sharpness the

120

pinnacle of Chhoba Bamare in the unsurveyed tract of country to the north-west of the Bhote Kosi. This 19,550-foot pinnacle must offer one of the most outstanding rock climbs in the world, and although its summit is on the frontier ridge it could most probably be reached from the Chyadu Khola, only one march beyond the point where we turned out of the Bhote Kosi to enter the Rolwaling Gorge.

Far below our feet was another enchanting new country beyond the Khimti Khola, its river hidden by the steepness of the jungle slopes hemming it; and what a magnificent surprise it was when we descended into it to discover that this glen was quite different from any other we had seen in Nepal. Instead of having to hunt for a camp spot there were acres of perfect turf to choose from—an expanse wide enough to land an aeroplane. Its very spaciousness gave a wonderful lift to the spirit.

But there came a further touch of magic when I went down to the river to wash, and was greeted by a flash of white wings and a series of shrill calls. The birds settled near me, and they turned out to be a small flock of ibis bills, rare waders from Tibet that we had glimpsed in the Rolwaling Gorge. Now I was close enough to distinguish to perfection the sharp curve of the slender red bill, the long legs, grey mantle and prominent black crescent markings on the chest. Like all waders they hardly kept still but made excited dashes hither and thither, finally flying off with frenzied shrill calls like so many redshank.

There was a most beautiful light that evening as the sun shed its soft light on the thundery cumulus floating on the green hillsides, changing it gradually from green to gold until every tree and stone shone with prickly brilliance. Almost imperceptibly the hard features softened till the landscape was no longer golden but pink, which changed almost in the same instant to an intense crimson—a dramatic light I have seen only

121

once before on green hills, and that was in 1948 in the Butter-
mere Valley in the Lake District, following a September rain-
storm. Now that the sun had set there was the same luminous
quality that there had been then, the silhouettes of rounded
hills merging into a green sky which was slowly filling with pale
stars.

What surprised us that night was how cold it was at this
height of only six or seven thousand feet, and we had to move
fast to keep warm when we struck camp at half-past five next
morning. Even the Sherpas were complaining of cold, and
the people we met on the path had their blankets round them
like shawls, with only their noses protruding.

In a short walk we came to Those—by far the neatest and
cleanest little clachan I have ever seen in India or Nepal. With
its cottages gleaming white and pink, and neatly paved paths
leading through the village, it made a great impression on us.
The shopkeepers were sitting waiting for business in their open
showrooms, and as this was the first shopping centre the Sherpas
and ourselves had seen for many weeks, a brisk business was
done.

As we looked around us we discovered that this was no
ordinary village, for at the back of many of the houses were
blacksmiths' shops, and when we looked in we saw ladles,
large spoons, matchets, kukris, etc., being hammered out. It
was coal and not coke that was being used for fires, though
where it came from I was unable to discover. The womenfolk
worked the bellows and the men beat out the implements on
stones specially hollowed and shaped as jigs. Wishing to have
some memento of the place we all bought razor-sharp kukris.

We were amused when we passed through the village to be
suddenly hailed from the loft of a house overlooking the path.
We looked in and saw a detachment of soldiers, some asleep,
some half-awake, with the guard commander doing his best to

straighten himself up in a manner befitting a soldier. As old soldiers ourselves, accustomed to sleeping off dull jobs, we could appreciate the situation, and what could be a nicer job then guarding this trade-route to Tibet? With hardly a clue about what he was doing the guard commander examined our documents, laboriously copied the wrong things into a book, and told us to proceed.

The march from here back to the Bhote Kosi across two passes was up to the high standard that had gone before, with a thrill at breakfast in the sight of three wall creepers—birds which we last saw in Garhwal at 17,000 feet. Here they were in their winter haunts in a little gully above a stream, but still clinging to walls as befitted their names. The wall creeper is a superb little bird, particularly when it flitters from one rock to another like a gaudy butterfly, flashing crimson, white and lavender. Its size is that of a starling, and even when its colours do not show vividly it is easy to recognise by reason of its square tail, curved bill and undulating flight. It is the same species that one finds high in the Alps in summer and at sea level in winter, and it interested me to discover that its vertical migration in the Himalaya is almost the same as in the Alps, 7,000 feet in the Himalaya corresponding to sea level in Europe.

One of the pleasantest parts of this walk was along a little glen through alpine meadows where little boys and girls were tending goats and sheep on the pastures. Wallowing in the streams were water buffaloes, and here and there were little parties of peasants cutting and harvesting fields of yellow rice. It was interesting to find that the people hereabouts keep bees, the hives being hollowed-out logs sealed at the end with clay.

The Sherpas were in their element, for there was plenty of chang to be had here, and in one place we watched them brew it up. Taking the fermented seeds of a plant they called morua, they wrapped them up in a large leaf to make a funnel filler; into the open end of the filler they poured clear water, which emerged at the other end as a milky fluid like dirty dishwater. This was the drink of their hearts' desire, and when we said that we preferred plain water they assured us that it was bad for us.

Finding a camp site convenient for water is not always as easy as might be imagined. There would be no difficulty of course if the Sherpas had their way, for they would simply pull into the nearest house. We made it a policy not to sleep in houses or camp in the vicinity of villages, for disease is all too easily caught by a European in these unhygienic parts. Accordingly, we used to split up our party in early afternoon, one sahib to stay with the Sherpas and urge them away from the chang pots, the others to press on and find a camp site providing fuel and water, and preferably with a good outlook.

Douglas' camp spot that night, though it drew complaints from the porters who had to climb 2,000 feet to reach it, was an inspired choice. We were in jungle, yet there was a view from it to the ridges we had crossed, with glimpses of the Rolwaling peaks to the north. Carving up our chicken round the camp fire that night our only regret was that this was among the last of our wild camps, for in two days' time we should be in Charikot and finished with this hill crossing. We knew we must cherish this last of the ridge camps, and it was well worth cherishing— especially at sunrise after a night of frost.

The speed of a Himalayan sunrise is a perpetual surprise. The date was 13th November, and when I looked out of the tent at five o'clock I looked over valleys and foothills submerged in darkness. Then quite suddenly there was a kindle of fire in the east, which spread into a glow of light and became a torch of flame casting a searchlight that picked out of shadow little dimples of mountain and turned the stream to silver. In another

124

instant the torch was a huge ball of fire and the trees were softly glowing as though with flames.

We would have liked to spend another day in this idyllic spot; instead we had to strike camp and press on over the next col to a corrie of terraced fields, with a maze of paths criss-crossing it. As Douglas, George and Tom were nowhere to be seen, and this was a place where they could easily take a wrong turning, I left Nyma and Kamin, who were most lightly laden, to wait for them and take them over the ridge to the Bhote Kosi, where I proposed to camp.

It was a joyful route—through varied terrain of fields, jungle and alps—to the crest of the ridge, where a sparrowhawk swooped on a bulbul and would have caught it but for our sudden appearance. Several thousand feet below I could see the bridge and the house where Tom had given medical aid to the sick man a couple of months earlier. The valley had then been vivid green with growing rice; now it was yellow with ripe grain from valley floor to the high corries.

The harvest was in full swing, and our first enquiries were for the headman we had doctored. To our relief we heard that he was fit and well. Chang was provided for us, and it was late afternoon by the time we dropped down to the glen and camped by the river. Unfortunately, by nightfall the other three had still not turned up at the camp site. This was disappointing, as I had a large meal waiting for them, and now they would need to spend a night out without food or bedding. I decided to go on to Charikot early next morning, since I felt fairly certain that they had taken a southern path by mistake and would cross the Bhote Kosi lower down, and thus reach Charikot by a different route.

Next morning I experienced something of the feeling of closeness to the Himalaya that I had felt for the Scottish Highlands during the solitary wanderings of my boyhood days; I felt this, especially in the early morning, when thin airships of cloud lay on the vast Rolwaling slopes as I climbed the ridge to Charikot, stopping now and then to look at the abyss of space between a valley floor and the pale spires in the sky, or listen to the songs of birds, the cries of bulbuls, or the screaming calls of green parakeets. There was much to see—brilliant yellow and red sunbirds, shrikes and bushchats, eagles and falcons.

I have sometimes thought that it would be an extraordinarily pleasant thing to go on a Himalayan expedition alone, with only a few chosen Sherpas as companions; not for anti-social reasons, but because of the simplicity of the whole thing. Not only could equipment and food be kept to a minimum, but one would be nearer the people, with a sharpened awareness of the country. One tends to lose consciousness of self when one is alone, and the magic of the mountains sinks in deeper. So the loss of my companions was something of a gain to me during those twenty-four hours.

The meadow at Charikot where I had half expected to find my three friends was deserted, and I went to the police post to make enquiries. The captain who had been so helpful a few weeks before was amusing in his enthusiasm at seeing me again, and insisted on holding hands and accompanying me wherever I went, looking earnestly into my face the while and beaming at my every remark. With a following of the whole village we returned to the meadow and put the camp in position. The crowd was dispersing when the missing trio walked in.

They had taken the southern route as I suspected and had been lucky to find an empty house to crawl into for the night, where they soon had a fire going—such a roaster in fact that they wakened in the night with the timbers of the ceiling smouldering and had to rush to the stream and carry water to dowse the flames. Apart from being hungry, they had spent a

126

comfortable night, and as soon as it was light they were on the move to a house to ask for food.

The owner of the house was an old sepoy, and he bade them sit down while rice was husked and guavas and bananas were plucked from the trees. Beginning with a mountain of rice, lentils, potatoes—all very highly spiced with chillies—they had then gone on to the guavas and bananas—the finest and biggest breakfast they had ever eaten. The idea of being able to pluck a meal from the trees and fields round the house intrigued them immensely.

Nyma was the sorrowful subject of our conversation that afternoon. We had discovered that he had been extracting a baksheesh from every porter we had engaged, which was the reason why the wage figure had been so high throughout the trip. We also had proof that he was swindling us on food, for though we had bought 180 rupees' worth of food in Namche to see us back to Katmandu, he now declared this was finished. As it was physically impossible for our party to have eaten the lot in such a short time we could only conclude that he had sold it. We decided to get him out of the way forthwith by making him messenger to the British Embassy at Katmandu to order up a lorry for us at Bhatgaon in five day's time.

Once he had gone we called a conference of the Sherpas and appointed Dawa Tenzing headman. It was dismaying to be told that Dawa was really our official headman, and that Nyma had usurped the post by his air of confidence, plus the fact that he had an odd word of English. Kharab Joe now piped up to say that the reason Nyma would not engage him as a Sherpa was that he refused to pay him his baksheesh. Every other porter admitted that he was paying Nyma half a rupee a day of our money. The great thing was that this plague to the expedition was now out of the way and we could settle down happily.

Next day we had a holiday and spent it with the Nepali captain, who turned up early to go on shikar with our gun. We thought we were fit until we tried to keep up with this lean man on a 2,000-foot slope. He had a lively sense of humour and knew he was forcing the sweat out of us. Panting and puffing, we were holding our own until the captain slipped off his shoes and literally ran away from us. But we had our revenge on the way down by leaving him standing. We could bound down easily in our rubber-soled boots while he had to take it more sedately, because his shoes had no nails in them and the stones were too sharp for fast running in bare feet. We could now tell him that the Nepalis were 'kharab wallahs,' since he had told us that was what we were on the way up.

As a shikar trip it was a washout. We shot nothing, though we did look down from the top of our peak into precipitous jungle, alive with bears, panther and deer, according to the captain. The best sight was a pallid harrier flashing black and white as it banked on long narrow wings high above the Bhote Kosi. That afternoon was our last at Charikot, and we could not help contrasting the view now with the view when we first arrived at this platform on the edge of our exploration area. Everything had been simplified into a misty blueness of distance by the press of monsoon clouds—a mysterious but featureless mountain wall. Now we could see and read in terms of human endeavour the complexity of rock ridges and icy peaks that stretched ahead to Tibet. These hidden treasures locked away in Rolwaling had been ours to seek, and we felt rich indeed to have found them.

All the beauty of the Himalaya seemed to be compressed before us as the warmth of evening overspread the glen of the Bhote Kosi and the vast slopes became tinged with pink. My camera stood on its tripod and I took photo after photo, trying hard to capture for ever this sequence of colour, snapping every few minutes the glow on peaks that were still ablaze after night had fallen in the valleys. It is then that one appreciates the height of the Himalaya, and the meaning of the word 'unearthly.'

The marches back were very different from our outward journey to Charikot. Then we had been sweltering in damp monsoon heat and had to drive unwilling bodies—our own, as well as a string of ne'er-do-well coolies. It had been the Dassera, when everything was green and flourishing after the life-giving rains. Now it was harvest festival, and the terraces were yellow with rice waiting to be cut or bare with stubble.

It was a Sunday when we left Charikot, and though the hour was sunrise the paths were busy with people in their gayest dress, the women in brightly-coloured saris with orange flowers in their hair, the men in tight pyjamas, silk shirts and cloth jackets of semi-European cut. Many carried offerings, for all were going to the temples to say their prayers and pay homage to Shiva or Buddha, or both.

Much to our joy we were greeted by some of our old Charikot coolies who had carried for us into Rolwaling. They gave us big salaams and even gave us presents of eggs and potatoes. They too were in their Sunday best and looked quite different from the ragged men who had lifted our crates so valiantly out of the Bhote Kosi and through jungle to the winter cold of Beding. One of them insisted on carrying my pack for a mile or two, and I felt I was losing a friend when I saw him go. By their deportment and general conduct these simple men expressed the best of mankind, unspoiled by greed, laziness or sophistication.

It was astonishing to see how the streams that had troubled us on the outward journey had shrunk—especially the Charnawati Khola, which had been a grey flood and had forced us to use combined tactics. We could now cross it dry shod. Even the long climbs from the river beds to the high ridges seemed to have shrunk, but the villages were more beautiful, for they were decked with ropes of flowers and cunningly ornamented with woven rice stalks and rosettes of ripened grain. Over temples and mountain streams were double strands of orange flowers, hung daisy-chain fashion like those we had seen in the Dudh Kosi. Every house seemed to take pride in its decorative stackyards.

That day we covered ground that had formerly taken two marches, and we camped at the end of it on our old 'swing camp' on the Sangasoti Danda. What a view had been hidden from us in the monsoon! Now we looked on the whole frontier ridge of Nepal from Annapurna past Manaslu and Gosianthan to Gauri Sankar. Far inside Tibet we could see swelling snow domes peeping over gaps in the jagged ridge. We were not taken in by that apparently simple mountain wall of 26,000 feet. Between us and it were rock barriers and jagged summits just visible against the crinkle of glaciers, revealing that there were intermediate valleys and gorges lying across the path of the explorer beyond the foothills.

We seemed to feel the pulse of the earth that night, as darkness deepened and a rich wave of fire lit the crest of the Himalaya, to be dowsed by the rim of the earth. The light of the sky ebbed visibly, in sharp pulsations, violet light deepening to envelope the pale peaks and bring a sparkle to the first stars.

There was a curious ceremony round the camp fire that night. Poor Ang Dawa had been unwell for several days, and although Tom had been doctoring him steadily, the medicine was having no effect. This good-looking youngster was not merely sick but quite ill, and daily we watched him grow weaker. Despite long prayers at every chorten we passed, and the tying of little prayer flags on every suitable pole, his supplications to Buddha were having no effect. We saw him go through many peculiar rites, from prostrations before small shrines to the offering of rice and grain.

Tonight there was something unusual afoot, as I saw when I went to the fire to look at a steamed pudding I was making in the pressure cooker. Ang Dawa stood with a bowl of rice in hand praying earnestly, touching his forehead with handfuls of the rice and scattering it at his side. Beside him stood Dawa Tenzing with a little tray on which had been set up candles and some little figures like plasticine puppets, cunningly manufactured from stiff tsampa dough. Without saying a word he held the tray out for my inspection.

The tray was arranged as a little stage, with the figure of a lama beside two chortens and an unlit candle. Between another two chortens and facing the lamas were the figures of a man and a woman. The Sherpas round the camp fire looked towards Ang Dawa, their lips moving in prayer with his. In the flickering firelight it was a strangely impressive scene, becoming invested with a touch of magic when rice was scattered on the flames and a burning brand was taken from the fire by a wild-looking Sherpa called Ang Phutar. With it he lit the candle on the tray. The sick man continued to pray while Dawa Tenzing walked slowly round the fire, the candle on his tray illuminating the strange little stage. Then he changed direction towards Namche Bazar, and at the same moment Ang Phutar with his burning brand seemed to go into a frenzy, slashing at the heels of Dawa and yelling fiendishly at the top of his voice. The devil tormenting the sick man was being driven back to Namche, and we assumed that the puppet set-up was meant to be a representation of the devil. Tray, puppets and candles must have been thrown away, for the party returned to the fire empty-handed.

After this there was a long series of prayers, sung rather than spoken, the chorus being punctuated with hand claps and

131

staccato passages marking changes of tempo. There must be a traditional pattern in all this, learned from a very early age, for every man knew his part. Unfortunately it did not cure Ang Dawa.

There was no frost that night but the dew was heavy, becoming vaporous as the sun drew it from the ground. The effect on the peaks was tremendous. Today they were soft, with colours in pastel shades—not the brazen, hard colours generally seen in the Himalaya at this time of year. We strode along the summit ridge of the Sangasoti, and every now and then we had to jerk our eyes upward to assure ourselves that these gauzy shapes over Tibet were real. Shooting out of grey cloud layers thousands of feet thick the peaks were hardly more tangible than the vapour which was gradually swallowing them up. They seemed to be too fantastically high to be real. This view gave us some idea of the true scale of the Nepal Himalaya, for we commanded a prospect from the foothills at 3,000 feet to the tops at over 26,000 in a distance of less than forty miles.

We realised then that one of the things we had been missing in the perfect weather that had been our almost daily lot was the variety of a changing atmosphere. Day after day we had been seeing row upon row of sparkling clear ice peaks, and had come to an almost blasé acceptance of them. In Garhwal the peaks had played a game of hide and seek with us to the end of a four and a half months' journey, surprising us when we least expected it by enthralling views that sent a leap to our hearts. Not that we were complaining of good weather, but one gets too used to it when every day is like the one that went before. Today we felt as if we were seeing the Himalaya for the first time, but the view did not last. By breakfast time the clouds had closed round the peaks, and we faced a 4,000-foot descent to the Sun Kosi, to camp that night in a ricefield barely 2,000 feet above sea level among a deafening chorus of cicadas.

132

The walk next day was strangely different from our memory of the upward journey. We remembered it for the first bathe of the expedition, when we had banished the feeling of torrid heat by floating blissfully in a pool of the deep river, as it flowed in a series of waterfalls through green ricefields. The river had practically disappeared and the fresh green of the rice had gone. The fields had been harvested and were now a neutral grey. But the calling of a sandpiper, and a sight of this little bird of the Scottish glens, sent our spirits up. There was a green sandpiper here as well, and a new bird for us was a rufus-bellied niltava—a superb little flycatcher of dark blue and yellow. Men,women and children were busy threshing and stacking the rice crop in the higher fields of this deep-trenched valley.

Our Sherpas were feeling the heat in this lower country, and Dawa raced round like a whippet, seeking out a chang-house in each village we passed through. He was taking his responsibilities as sirdar very well and kept us informed of his intentions. If he said he was breaking off for half an hour, then half an hour it was, not longer. He never argued when we gave him an order, and there was a happy spirit about our party that made the daily marches a joy.

Unfortunately, this was our last camp of the march, for on the other side of the ridge were Dhulikhel and Banepa, where we expected to catch the lorry next day. As though in honour of it Mingma put on his last great feed for us—a roast chicken done to perfection. And I finished it off by making the last giant dumpling.

Sunrise next morning might have been in the Highlands—a red sky softly glowing on purple hills with banners of pearly sky resting on their shoulders, until the sun burst clear in a ball of fire, dispelling the illusion in a far harder light than ever we see in the Highlands.

A short walk across a ridge led us down to the houses of Dhulikhel, where Gurkha soldiers were drilling on an alp commanding a view of the snows. This square of green was the perfect place for breakfast, and in no time we were surrounded by vendors selling bananas, eggs, milk, firewood, etc. Between the four of us we ate for this one meal over a hundred small sweet bananas, and suffered no ill effects!

The Vale of Katmandu now lay below us, and all that remained was to walk down to the town of Banepa, which marked the end of the expedition for us. Beside the smartly dressed Nepalis that crowded the streets of this Newar city our rough Sherpas looked a different race indeed, and the sophisticated Nepalis looked curiously at their quaint homespuns and long pigtails.

At eleven o'clock we were picked up by lorry, and for some of the Sherpas who had never even seen a motor vehicle, let alone been on one, the most exciting part of the journey was still to come. It must have been an extraordinary experience for them as we scraped the walls of houses and crushed through narrow lanes never meant for motor vehicles, with chickens and pigs flying for their lives. But they were enjoying it, and the eyes of those who had never seen a town before were big with wonder as we whisked through the streets of Katmandu by roundabouts, statues and electric cables, to swing into the Embassy grounds and pull up before its magnificent pillared front.

What a welcome the ambassador and his wife and staff gave us! We had expected to camp or go to the Government Rest House. Instead we were plied with mugs of foaming beer and each given a suite of luxurious rooms. It all seemed too good to be true, especially when a bag of mail was put into our hands and we relaxed in armchairs to read. It is good to be denied the comforts of civilisation if only to savour them again after abstinence, and how Mr and Mrs Summerhayes spoiled us with huge meals, wines, and morning tea in bed!

We spent four happy days as guests at the Embassy, being taken by car to see something of the wonders of Katmandu and Patan. We visited the lovely temple of Machendranath, whose three elegant storeys stand in a spacious grove of eucalyptus trees and house the god that brings rain to the thirsting crops before the monsoon. He is brought out in June in an elaborate chariot and worshipped by Hindus and Buddhists alike. If the rains have not come they are bound to do so when he is brought out.

Most impressive to me was the Buddhist shrine of Swayambhunath, which crowns a pointed hill top. A gilded spire springs from a summit tower painted with huge eyes meant to portray the all-seeing eye of Buddha. The climb up to it leads through an avenue of giant Buddhas and up an imposing staircase of 500 steps, alive with monkeys. Swarming everywhere, old, young and infants in arms, the stench of these red monkeys was rather revolting. Drums were beating and bells ringing as we climbed up, while dogs and monkeys fought over votive offerings left in the temple. Hindus as well as Buddhists worship here, among a galaxy of smaller shrines representing a variety of gods.

From these gilt carvings glowing in the sunshine we looked over the flat Vale of Nepal, amazed to realise that every field of its great expanse is turned by hand. Now it was mostly dun-coloured where the soil had been turned after the rice harvest, but near the winding river were plots of brilliant green where potatoes and vegetables grew. Rice, wheat, potatoes, ground nuts, pulse, maize, sugar cane, buckwheat, chillies and pumpkins are the main crops of the valley. Most of the agricultural work is done by the Newars, who are also the shopkeepers and traders of Katmandu, with branches of their clan at Lhasa for handling the Tibetan trade. Now that brains are more important than brawn in Nepal it will be interesting to see if the Newars rise again to their old position of being a power in the land. The tendency is already shaping that way, but Nepal is a land of intrigue, and no one can forecast the future. The main occupation of the Gurkhas is still military service, such things as politics being well beyond their scope. Nor is there such a thing as compulsory education in Nepal, though this must come in the near future.

Quite a number of Americans had arrived in Katmandu since our leaving. Most of them had been sent over in an advisory capacity under United Nations auspices, and were studying problems of health, agriculture, sanitation, etc., to report on what could be done to make Nepal a more productive and healthier country. Roads, communications, mechanised farming methods, war on mosquitoes, were some of the problems they were investigating. They had a cinema, and each day it was showing news and documentary films in a drive to let the people of Nepal see how much better their country could be to live in.

There was no doubt that the experts were doing their jobs with thoroughness. One medical man and his wife had just returned from a tour of the Terai by elephant, and he was proposing to teach the jungle dwellers there how to use DDT sprays in an attempt to eradicate the malarial diseases which at present drastically reduce the average length of life. Another man we met on horseback was just returning from 'up country,' where he had been looking at a 'cattle ranch.' Still another was inspecting the valley fields to work out the best type of mechanical plough for tilling the soil. Others were working on communications, and I heard a plan for getting together a 'voters' roll' for the whole of Nepal, a scheme which would come as a shock to the hill people, who would discover for the first time in their lives that they are citizens of a foreign country. They do not regard themselves as belonging to Nepal. Nepal to them means the far-off country of Katmandu and its surrounding flat land.

Yet at what speed do events move nowadays. A way of life that has lasted hundreds of years has changed dramatically in less than a decade. How could Dr Longstaff have forecast, for example, that his chapter on Nepal in *This My Voyage* would be out of date by the time it appeared in print? Take the sentence: 'Mysterious Pokra, tropical, low-lying by a lake and closely backed by the immense peaks of Annapurna, is still beyond our ken.' Annapurna was climbed in 1950, the year the book came out, and in 1953 an air service was established at Pokra, where two medical missionaries are now at work. The veil of mystery is not being merely withdrawn but rent apart. Hillary's expedition in 1954 climbed twenty-three peaks in the course of a single season, mapping and exploring the region east of Everest, while national expeditions in other parts of the range were attacking the great peaks of Manaslu and Dhaulagiri. Cho Oyu (26,750 feet) was climbed, Gauri Sankar was attempted, and as I write the Nepal face of Kanchenjunga has just been climbed—the greatest piece of mountaineering in this century— Tom MacKinnon having played no inconsiderable part in its conquest. A sign that we ourselves were not a moment too soon in entering Nepal was the arrival of seven bulldozers across the Chandrigiri Pass, the first vehicles ever to arrive in Katmandu under their own power.

The pleasant time at the Embassy passed all too swiftly, listening to symphonies and fragments from operas played on long-playing records, and being royally entertained. The only black spot was dealing with Nyma the notorious. Now that we had an interpreter we could tax him with his disloyalty in financial matters. He had to be taught his lesson, if only for the benefit of future travellers, and having said our say we deducted a large number of rupees from his pay to teach him a lesson in honesty. When he appealed to the other Sherpas they turned their backs on him, which was proof enough to us that we were doing the right thing, however repellent it was to be so firm with him.

The plan now was to leave Katmandu and climb as far as the Chandrigiri Pass, to arrive there at sunset and spend one last night within sight of the snows. The path was as busy as Sauchiehall Street, with Indian sappers and coolies toiling to prepare a way of descent for the bulldozers, which were now over the col and facing the worst part of the route. Landslides had already taken place at one or two points, and we had to keep a sharp look-out for falling stones, which whizzed through the air and bounded through the trees, indicating what would happen to an out-of-control bulldozer.

It was a relief to get clear of all this and climb along the ridge to camp in a small clearing, looking over a gossamer cloud sea whose tide was gradually filling the Vale of Katmandu and chilling the air around us with damp.

The view we had hoped for was reserved for the next night, when we least expected it. Three thousand feet below us was the road-head where we would catch a lorry to take us to the railway, but there was a little peak that looked as if it might give some sort of view, and we climbed to it.

Instead of a little view, a vast panorama was spread before us —ridge upon ridge mounting in grey blue to become the frozen crest of the Himalaya. Laid out before us was the route of our journey, signposted by Gauri Sankar and the square-cut flank of Rolwaling beneath which had been our base camp. We filled our eyes with it, imprinting it on our memories, conscious that tomorrow it would be only a memory, but one to treasure to the end of our days.